CoffeeScript Application Development

Write code that is easy to read, effortless to maintain, and even more powerful than JavaScript

Ian Young

PUBLISHING

BIRMINGHAM - MUMBAI

CoffeeScript Application Development

First published: August 2013

Production Reference: 1200813

Published by Packt Publishing Ltd.
Livery Place
35 Livery Street
Birmingham B3 2PB, UK.

ISBN 978-1-78216-266-7

www.packtpub.com

Cover Image by Aniket Sawant (aniket_sawant_photography@hotmail.com)

Credits

Author
Ian Young

Reviewers
Becker
Adam Bronte
Enrique Vidal

Acquisition Editor
Martin Bell

Lead Technical Editor
Ankita Shashi

Technical Editors
Dipika Gaonkar
Aparna K
Pragati Singh
Aniruddha Vanage

Project Coordinator
Kranti Berde

Proofreader
Mario Cecere

Indexer
Tejal Soni

Production Coordinator
Prachali Bhiwandkar

Cover Work
Prachali Bhiwandkar

About the Author

Ian Young wrote his very first program on a TI-89 scientific calculator — an infinite loop that printed an insulting message to one of his friends. As one might expect, things could only improve from there. Ian graduated from Grinnell College with a degree in Computer Science, and since then has been working as a web developer for small tech companies; first in Minneapolis and now in San Diego. He loves web technology, small teams, frequent iteration, testing, beautiful ideas, free speech, free beer, and any tool that reduces cognitive overhead.

Acknowledgements

Katherine, for putting up with my stupid face.

My reviewers and editors, for finding all of my mistakes.

Photos, my favorite part of the book:

- Steve Jurvetson (https://flickr.com/photos/jurvetson/2229899)
- Rosalia Wilhelm (https://commons.wikimedia.org/wiki/File:Widderkaninchen.JPG)

Open source software, without which none of this would be possible:

- Jeremy Ashkenas, CoffeeScript (http://coffeescript.org/)
- Ryan Dahl, Node (http://nodejs.org/)
- Isaac Z. Schlueter, npm (https://github.com/isaacs/npm)
- Dustin Diaz, reqwest (https://github.com/ded/reqwest)
- Tilde, Inc., RSVP.js (https://github.com/tildeio/rsvp.js)
- David Heinemeier Hansson, Rails (http://rubyonrails.org/)
- Brunch team, Brunch (http://brunch.io/)
- TJ Holowaychuk, Express (http://expressjs.com/)
- Andrew Dunkman, connect-assets (https://github.com/adunkman/connect-assets)

About the Reviewers

Adam Bronte is a well-versed software developer expert on web technologies. He is the co-founder and CTO of the pet services company, Furlocity. With over six years of experience in the industry, Adam has worked on all aspects of software development.

Enrique Vidal is a Software Engineer from Tijuana. He has worked on web development and system administration for many years, he is now focusing on Ruby and CoffeeScript development.

He has been fortunate to work with great developers such as this book's author, in different companies in the United States and México. He enjoys the challenge of coding payment systems, online invoicing, social networking applications, and so on. He is keen on helping startups at an early stage and actively supporting a few open source projects.

> I'd like to thank Packt and the author for allowing me to be part of this book's technical reviewer team.

www.PacktPub.com

Support files, eBooks, discount offers and more

You might want to visit www.PacktPub.com for support files and downloads related to your book.

Did you know that Packt offers eBook versions of every book published, with PDF and ePub files available? You can upgrade to the eBook version at www.PacktPub.com and as a print book customer, you are entitled to a discount on the eBook copy. Get in touch with us at service@packtpub.com for more details.

At www.PacktPub.com, you can also read a collection of free technical articles, sign up for a range of free newsletters and receive exclusive discounts and offers on Packt books and eBooks.

http://PacktLib.PacktPub.com

Do you need instant solutions to your IT questions? PacktLib is Packt's online digital book library. Here, you can access, read and search across Packt's entire library of books.

Why Subscribe?

- Fully searchable across every book published by Packt
- Copy and paste, print and bookmark content
- On demand and accessible via web browser

Free Access for Packt account holders

If you have an account with Packt at www.PacktPub.com, you can use this to access PacktLib today and view nine entirely free books. Simply use your login credentials for immediate access.

Table of Contents

Preface

If you do web development, chances are you've at least *heard* of CoffeeScript. Though it's less than five years old, this little language has received a lot of attention, and it's getting harder to ignore. Maybe you've already worked with it a little bit, or maybe you're just wondering what the fuss is all about. Good news! CoffeeScript is a delightful language that can help you write better code and have fun doing it. In this book, we will explore the language itself, and find out first-hand how it can help us build beautiful web applications.

What is CoffeeScript?

CoffeeScript is a programming language. Like most programming languages, it offers control structures to describe the logic of our application, simple data types to store and manipulate information, and functions to encapsulate sections of program execution.

What makes CoffeeScript special is the way it is compiled. When most languages are compiled, they are translated into **machine code**—low-level instructions to the computer's processor. CoffeeScript is different: when compiled, it is instead translated *into JavaScript*. We write CoffeeScript code, give it to the CoffeeScript compiler and receive JavaScript code as output. This output can then be passed to anything that consumes JavaScript, such as a browser, or a standalone JavaScript interpreter.

This technique, dubbed **transcompilation**, allows us to use an alternative language on platforms that only directly support JavaScript. Client-side web development is the most prominent example, since JavaScript is the only supported general-purpose scripting solution on most web browsers. Other platforms such as Node.js and Rhino also offer useful features, but expect JavaScript input. JavaScript is nothing if not prolific, and CoffeeScript allows us to make use of all that existing tooling, but to write our code in a different language.

Why CoffeeScript?

CoffeeScript was certainly not the first (or last) language to target JavaScript platforms. Many established languages, such as Ruby, Python, C, and Java have one or more projects focused on compiling that language to JavaScript. And other languages have been developed specifically to target JavaScript—notably Dart, TypeScript, and Coco.

 The CoffeeScript wiki itself maintains an extensive list of other languages that compile to JavaScript. You can find it at `https://github.com/jashkenas/coffee-script/wiki/List-of-languages-that-compile-to-JS`.

While it's not alone in its approach, CoffeeScript has seen the most success of any language that compiles to JavaScript. It is the tenth most popular language on GitHub, it ships by default with Ruby on Rails, and it has large followings in both client-side and server-side developer communities.

So what makes CoffeeScript special? Just like Goldilocks and her pilfered porridge, CoffeeScript derives its strength from being *just right*. It is a marked improvement over JavaScript; we'll spend much of this book learning how CoffeeScript can help us write code that is more concise, easier to read, and less prone to bugs. However, CoffeeScript does not overreach on features. CoffeeScript has little to no runtime of its own—there is no extra metadata to track, no extra memory management, no non-standard data structures. Instead, CoffeeScript compiles directly to ordinary-looking JavaScript, much like what an experienced JavaScript developer might write. In fact, CoffeeScript is less a new language than it is a shorthand for easily expressing the best practices of JavaScript.

CoffeeScript is an eminently pragmatic language, and this is the secret to its success. It's easy for JavaScript developers to learn, and most expertise carries over. It doesn't incur performance penalties over plain JavaScript. CoffeeScript and JavaScript can coexist peacefully, so it's easy to introduce CoffeeScript into existing JavaScript projects. Perhaps most importantly, CoffeeScript avoids the "magic" that is so often a source of bugs when the developer's assumptions don't match the language designer's assumptions. With CoffeeScript, it's very easy to understand what the resulting JavaScript will do and how it will behave.

It might also help that CoffeeScript is *fun*.

What this book covers

Chapter 1, Running a CoffeeScript Program, will cover installing the CoffeeScript tools and running a simple CoffeeScript program in both the console and a web browser.

Chapter 2, Writing Your First Lines of CoffeeScript, will explore the syntax of CoffeeScript and how it compiles to JavaScript.

In *Chapter 3, Building a Simple Application*, we will build an interactive web application and learn a few more CoffeeScript features along the way.

Chapter 4, Improving Our Application, will add more features to our web application, and explore more powerful CoffeeScript syntax.

Chapter 5, Using Classes, will teach us all about classes in CoffeeScript. It will also cover how to use them, how they work, and how to integrate with popular JavaScript frameworks.

In *Chapter 6, Refactoring with Classes*, we will use the new skills from previous chapter to refactor our web application using class-based structures.

In *Chapter 7, Advanced CoffeeScript Features*, we will learn advanced CoffeeScript features and idioms that reduce errors and make our code easier to understand. We will use them to add more features to our web application.

Chapter 8, Going Asynchronous, will show how CoffeeScript can help us deal with asynchronous operations, and integrate a third-party JavaScript library into our CoffeeScript application.

In *Chapter 9, Debugging*, we will learn how to use source maps to track problems in our application all the way back to the CoffeeScript source.

Chapter 10, Using CoffeeScript in More Places, will cover how to integrate CoffeeScript compilation into several popular web application frameworks.

In *Chapter 11, CoffeeScript on the Server*, we will run CoffeeScript on the server with Node.js, and learn how to integrate it with standard JavaScript Node modules.

What you need for this book

All you need for this book is a text editor and a working CoffeeScript compiler, and don't worry about the compiler — we'll cover installation and use of that tool in the first chapter! We provide instructions for using the tools on Windows, Mac OS X, and Linux. We'll be spending a lot of the book working on a client-side web application, so if you have any favorite development tools, feel free to bring those along. You'll also need a modern browser. The most recent version of Firefox or Chrome is ideal, but any other up-to-date browser such as Safari, Opera, or a *recent* Internet Explorer will also work fine.

Who this book is for

Some familiarity with the JavaScript language will help — CoffeeScript is a close relative, so it's useful to understand what the compiler's output is doing. It's also helpful, though not necessary, to have some experience with client-side web development. We'll be building a web application with a lot of CoffeeScript, plus a little HTML and CSS.

No experience with CoffeeScript is necessary. We'll cater to everyone from the total newbie to the person who has hacked together some CoffeeScript already but wants a better grasp of what's going on and how to best utilize the language.

Conventions

In this book, you will find a number of styles of text that distinguish between different kinds of information. Here are some examples of these styles, and an explanation of their meaning.

Code words in text are shown as follows: "We can pull in another module by using the `require` function."

A block of code is set as follows:

```coffeescript
fibonacci = (n) ->
  if n is 0 or n is 1
    n
  else
    fibonacci(n-1) + fibonacci(n-2)
```

When we wish to draw your attention to a particular part of a code block, the relevant lines or items are set in bold:

```
fibonacci = (n) ->
  if n is 0 or n is 1
    n
  else
    fibonacci(n-1) + fibonacci(n-2)
```

Any command-line input or output is written as follows:

```
coffee --compile --watch *.coffee
```

New terms and **important words** are shown in bold. Words that you see on the screen, in menus or dialog boxes for example, appear in the text like this: "clicking the **Next** button moves you to the next screen".

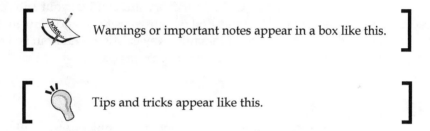

Warnings or important notes appear in a box like this.

Tips and tricks appear like this.

Reader feedback

Feedback from our readers is always welcome. Let us know what you think about this book—what you liked or may have disliked. Reader feedback is important for us to develop titles that you really get the most out of.

To send us general feedback, simply send an e-mail to feedback@packtpub.com, and mention the book title via the subject of your message.

If there is a topic that you have expertise in and you are interested in either writing or contributing to a book, see our author guide on www.packtpub.com/authors.

Customer support

Now that you are the proud owner of a Packt book, we have a number of things to help you to get the most from your purchase.

Downloading the example code

You can download the example code files for all Packt books you have purchased from your account at http://www.packtpub.com. If you purchased this book elsewhere, you can visit http://www.packtpub.com/support and register to have the files e-mailed directly to you.

Errata

Although we have taken every care to ensure the accuracy of our content, mistakes do happen. If you find a mistake in one of our books—maybe a mistake in the text or the code—we would be grateful if you would report this to us. By doing so, you can save other readers from frustration and help us improve subsequent versions of this book. If you find any errata, please report them by visiting http://www.packtpub.com/submit-errata, selecting your book, clicking on the **errata submission form** link, and entering the details of your errata. Once your errata are verified, your submission will be accepted and the errata will be uploaded on our website, or added to any list of existing errata, under the Errata section of that title. Any existing errata can be viewed by selecting your title from http://www.packtpub.com/support.

Piracy

Piracy of copyright material on the Internet is an ongoing problem across all media. At Packt, we take the protection of our copyright and licenses very seriously. If you come across any illegal copies of our works, in any form, on the Internet, please provide us with the location address or website name immediately so that we can pursue a remedy.

Please contact us at copyright@packtpub.com with a link to the suspected pirated material.

We appreciate your help in protecting our authors, and our ability to bring you valuable content.

Questions

You can contact us at questions@packtpub.com if you are having a problem with any aspect of the book, and we will do our best to address it.

1
Running a CoffeeScript Program

The very first thing we need to do in order to start using CoffeeScript is to install CoffeeScript itself. This will give us access to the CoffeeScript compiler, which we'll use to compile our beautiful CoffeeScript code into JavaScript that can be run in a browser (or other JavaScript environment). By the end of this chapter we'll be completely set up and ready to work.

There are a couple of steps involved in installing CoffeeScript. I know you're impatient to dive right into this great new language—who can blame you? But we'll have to stick it out through a little bit of system configuration. If we do so, we'll be rewarded with a stable CoffeeScript setup that works flawlessly and doesn't take any more of our attention.

In this chapter we will:

- Install the software that you need to run CoffeeScript code
- Learn how to use the software to run CoffeeScript, both from the command line and in a browser
- Use our new abilities to write a simple web application using CoffeeScript

Installing Node.js

To run CoffeeScript, first you'll need to install Node.js. Don't worry! If you don't want to learn Node.js, you won't need to. We just need to have the platform installed because the CoffeeScript compiler uses it.

If you get stuck at any point while installing or using Node.js, the IRC channel is a great place to look for help. You can use your IRC client of choice to connect to the #node.js room in irc. freenode.net, or you can connect through a web browser by visiting `http://webchat.freenode.net/?channels=node.js`.

Node.js (or simply **Node**) is a platform for running JavaScript at a low level, using the powerful and fast V8 engine. It's primarily used for web development, allowing developers to write the server side components of web applications in JavaScript. Node's most notable innovation is that it's highly non-blocking. Any system call that needs to wait for a result (such as network requests and disk reads) uses a callback, so Node can service another request while it waits for an operation to finish. This way of thinking meshes nicely with web applications which do a lot of network interaction, and it provides a lot of bang for your hardware buck. While we'll be using CoffeeScript to build a client side application, it works great with Node as well. We'll show you more about that in *Chapter 11, CoffeeScript on the Server*. The CoffeeScript compiler is written entirely in CoffeeScript and runs on Node. If you're curious, you can find the annotated CoffeeScript source on `http://coffeescript.org/`.

Installing Node.js on OS X

The Node project provides several options for installation on Mac OS X. The simplest method is the universal installer. If you don't already use a package management system for your development tools, you should use the installer. If you use **Homebrew** or **MacPorts** to manage your system and would like to install Node through those, follow the instructions for your package manager instead.

If for some reason none of these methods work for you, see the *Compiling Node.js manually* section. However, this is more difficult and not recommended unless you really need it.

Using the installer

The Node project provides a universal installer for Mac OS X. Visit `http://nodejs.org/download/`, and look for **Macintosh Installer**.

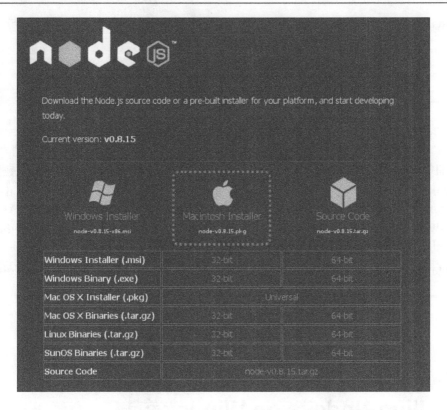

Download that file and double-click on it. Follow the prompts to install Node on your system.

Using Homebrew

Homebrew is a popular package management system for OS X. It maintains installed packages in a completely separate directory from the OS X system files, and offers easy package management from the command line. Homebrew offers an easy-to-use **formula** system to create new package definitions, and as a result offers a very large collection of user-contributed recipes.

Early versions of the Node package on Homebrew suffered from numerous bugs. Recent versions have received far fewer complaints and should be acceptable for our needs. Still, if you encounter serious problems using Node from Homebrew, consider uninstalling it and using the universal installer instead.

To install Node using Homebrew, simply use the command-line installer as follows:

```
brew install node
```

 For help with Homebrew, visit the official site at
http://mxcl.github.com/homebrew/.

Using Macports

MacPorts is another package management system for OS X. Like Homebrew, it maintains installed packages separately from the OS X system files. MacPorts is an older project, and is modeled on the BSD **ports** system. While it has been waning in popularity in recent years, it still has a large user base.

To install Node using MacPorts, simply use the command-line installer as follows:

```
sudo port install nodejs
```

 For help with MacPorts, visit the official site at
https://www.macports.org/.

Installing Node.js on Windows

There are several convenient installation options for Node on Windows. The method recommended for most people is to use the installer. If you cannot install software on your machine, or for other reasons wish to isolate Node, you can use the standalone executable instead. Finally, if you are already using the third-party package manager Chocolatey to manage packages on your machine, you may install Node through that system.

Using the installer

The Node project provides an install file for Windows systems. Visit http://nodejs.org/download/, and look for **Windows Installer**:

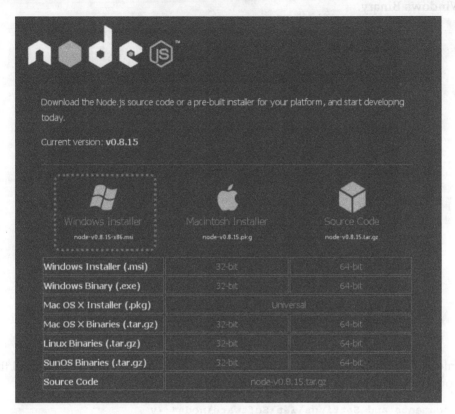

Download that file and double-click on it. Follow the prompts to install Node on your system.

Using the standalone executable

The Node project provides a `node.exe` file that you may download and call without installing anything on your system. Visit `http://nodejs.org/download/`, and look for **Windows Binary**.

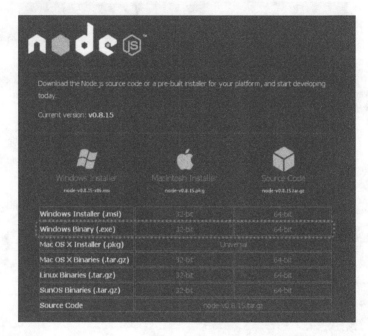

Download that file and put it in a directory you'll remember. Now you can call the file from the command line using the full path, as follows:

```
"C:\Documents and Settings\Ian\Software\node" -v
```

To save yourself some typing, you'll probably want to add that directory to your path. Once you do that, you can just call `node` without the full path.

 If you don't know how to add directories to your path, you can find instructions at `http://www.computerhope.com/issues/ch000549.htm`.

Using Chocolatey

Chocolatey is a package management system for Windows based on **NuGet** and **Powershell**. It is modeled on package managers for other systems, but is designed to deal with the Windows environment. It provides simple installation of many developer tools and libraries.

To install Node using Chocolatey, simply use the command-line installer:

```
cinst nodejs.install
```

 For help with Chocolatey, visit the official site at http://chocolatey.org/.

Installing Node.js on Linux

The easiest way to install Node on Linux is to use the package manager for your particular distribution. Most distributions offer a Node package, which will save the trouble of building it manually. If your distribution does not offer a Node package, see the *Compiling Node.js manually* section at the end of this chapter.

Using a graphical package manager

If you have a graphical utility to manage your system, such as Ubuntu Software Center or Synaptic, you can use that. Open the program and search for "**nodejs**". You will see a result similar to the following screenshot. Choose **Install** and wait until it informs you that it is finished.

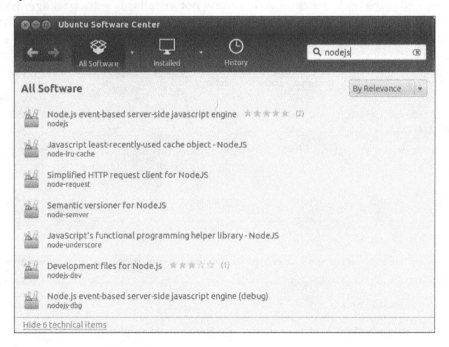

Using the command line

If you don't have a graphical utility, that's not a cause for alarm. Many distributions still use a command line tool to manage packages. Start by opening up a terminal. The exact commands to install Node depend on your package manager. Here are some of the more common options.

 If you can't find your distribution listed here, try the Node.js wiki at https://github.com/joyent/node/wiki/Installing-Node. js-via-package-manager.

Linux Mint/Ubuntu 12.04 (Precise Pangolin)

Ubuntu, Mint, and other distributions based on Debian unstable can use the venerable apt-get command-line tool to install Node.

```
sudo apt-get install nodejs
```

Debian Sid/Ubuntu 12.10 (Quantal Quetzal)

Systems using cutting-edge Debian packages can install Node with apt-get as stated earlier. However, you may also want to install the nodejs-legacy package, which provides the node executable. If you do not install this extra package, you will need to invoke Node on the command line with nodejs instead of node (this change was introduced to deal with a conflict between two different packages that both provide a node executable).

```
sudo apt-get install nodejs nodejs-legacy
```

Arch Linux

Arch Linux offers an official Node package, which may be installed using the pacman command-line tool:

```
sudo pacman -S nodejs
```

Fedora

Node is available in Fedora 18 and later versions. Install it through the package manager:

```
sudo yum install npm
```

If you are using an older Fedora release, see the following section.

Compiling Node.js manually

If you cannot install Node using one of the methods listed earlier, you may be able to compile it from source. This will work on most UNIX-like systems (including Mac OSX, Linux, and BSD). You may need some perseverance—compiling software from source often involves a few hiccups along the way. Remember, if you get stuck, a search engine is your best friend.

 For more information and solutions to some common problems, visit the Node wiki page on installation at `https://github.com/joyent/node/wiki/Installation`.

First let's install the dependencies we'll need to build Node. These include a **C++** compiler, the **make** build tool, and **Python** (which is used in the build process).

```
sudo apt-get install python g++ make
```

 The exact method you use to install the dependencies will vary based on your operating system. The commands shown should work for Debian based systems, including Ubuntu and Linux Mint. OS X users will need to install Xcode, and then install the Command Line Tools through Xcode.

Now we need to download the Node source code. Visit `http://nodejs.org/download/` and choose **Source Code**. Save it to somewhere you can remember, say ~/Downloads.

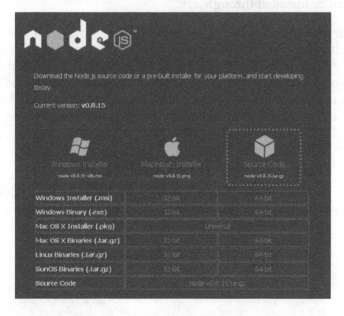

Let's visit the directory where you saved the file and unpack it. Note that the filename will have a version number in it that may be different from what is printed on the screenshot and in the command-line instructions.

```
cd ~/Downloads
tar xzvf node-v0.8.15.tar.gz
cd node-v0.8.15/
```

Now we'll prepare, build, and install Node. Be patient — these commands can take a while to complete!

```
./configure
sudo make install
```

These commands may throw errors if they don't find everything they need on your system. Read the error messages carefully. If you can't figure it out on your own, try searching online with the text of the error messages. Often you will find an existing post with a solution to the problem you are encountering.

Skipping the Node installation step

On certain systems, it may be possible to install CoffeeScript as a system package, rather than installing Node first as we are doing. For example, older versions of Homebrew offered a `coffeescript` package, and Ubuntu provides a CoffeeScript package that can be installed through `apt`.

However, these packages may be buggy or out-of-date, and you may find it difficult to control which version of the CoffeeScript package you are using. You will be at the mercy of a package maintainer (who may not even be actively updating the package any more). I *strongly* encourage you to follow the process detailed in the earlier sections of this chapter . Once you have installed Node, it will be very easy to manage your CoffeeScript installation, and you'll be glad you took this route.

Testing our Node installation

Let's make sure your Node installation is working properly. Check the version number with `node -v`. We will be shown a version number, as follows:

```
node -v
v0.8.15
```

Now let's open up the Node console. This is an interactive tool that lets you run JavaScript right from your command line! It can be very helpful if you want to try out small ideas in code and receive immediate feedback. We'll see later that CoffeeScript provides an equivalent console.

Run this:

```
node
```

You will be presented with a prompt. Try entering some JavaScript code, and hit *Enter* to execute.

```
> "Hello, world!"
'Hello, world!'
> var x = 3 + 7
undefined
> x / 2
5
```

Downloading the example code

You can download the example code files for all Packt books you have purchased from your account at http://www.packtpub.com. If you purchased this book elsewhere, you can visit http://www.packtpub.com/support and register to have the files e-mailed directly to you.

Testing npm

We'll also check if **npm** is installed. npm is the Node package manager. It is a set of utilities for installing and managing tools and libraries written for Node. It is backed by https://npmjs.org/, the official online repository for Node packages. Almost any public code written for Node will be published in the repository and can be installed seamlessly with a single npm command.

If you have version 0.6.3 or above of Node, it comes with npm automatically. If you are still in the Node console, hit *Ctrl + D* to close it and return to your regular command line.

```
npm -v
```

If you see a version number, you have npm and can continue on to the next step.

 If you don't have npm installed, the best way to get it is to upgrade to a recent version of Node following the instructions stated earlier. If you really cannot upgrade your version of Node, follow the installation instructions at https://github.com/isaacs/npm/.

Installing CoffeeScript

Hang in there! We're almost done. Now that we have installed Node, it's easy to install CoffeeScript.

```
npm install -g coffee-script
```

 If this command fails with a permissions error (which is sometimes reported as an EACCES error), you may need to run it with sudo, as follows:

```
sudo npm install -g coffee-script
```

This depends on the permissions of your Node installation, and varies between different systems.

Now you should be able to see a version number when you run the following command:

```
coffee -v
```

If so, congratulations! You've installed CoffeeScript!

 If you have trouble installing or using CoffeeScript, the IRC channel is a great place to look for help. You can use your IRC client of choice to connect to the #coffeescript room in irc.freenode.net, or you can connect through a web browser by visiting at http://webchat.freenode.net/?channels=coffeescript.

Our very first CoffeeScript code

Let's open up a CoffeeScript console. We saw earlier that Node provides a console to interactively run JavaScript code. You guessed it, the CoffeeScript console works the same way, but with CoffeeScript!

```
coffee
coffee> subject = "World"
'World'
coffee> "Hello, #{subject}!"
'Hello, World!'
```

Don't worry about the syntax for now. We'll get to that soon. When you're finished, hit *Ctrl + D* to close the console, and take a moment to bask in the glow of a properly configured development environment.

Compiling from a CoffeeScript file

Now that you've tried out the CoffeeScript console, let's try compiling a file. The console is great for trying out ideas and rapidly getting feedback from your code, but you'll do most of your work in CoffeeScript files, which you then compile to JavaScript.

Let's start with a very simple CoffeeScript file. CoffeeScript conventionally uses the .coffee extension, so let's name our file setup.coffee.

```
alert "Welcome!"
```

 The first thing that might jump out at you in this code is the lack of parentheses. In CoffeeScript parentheses are optional when calling a function, unless the function takes no arguments, or they are needed to resolve ambiguity.

Now let's compile this file to JavaScript. Run this from your terminal, in the same directory that holds setup.coffee:

```
coffee -c setup.coffee
```

The -c option tells the coffee executable that instead of opening a console, you wish to compile a file. You should now have a file in the same directory named setup.js. This is the result of your compilation. Open it, and you'll see JavaScript code. You might be able to guess what it will look like:

```
alert("Welcome!");
```

The CoffeeScript compiler usually creates very readable output (probably more readable than the output of a few programmers you know!). This is a great feature, because it means that if at any time you want to check the compiler's work, or debug, or explore how the compiler achieves something, you can simply open the compiled file in your favorite text editor and read through it. We'll make use of this throughout the book, especially in the next chapter. Be careful though—any changes you make to the JavaScript file will be overwritten the next time you compile. Treat the JavaScript output as read-only.

 While working through the examples, you may see output from your compiler that is slightly different from that printed here. Different versions of CoffeeScript will produce subtle variations in output. These differences are usually superficial, so don't be alarmed. If you compare the two side by side, you will usually be able to find the difference and see that the rest of the code is unchanged.

CoffeeScript support in the editor

Let's add support for CoffeeScript to your favorite text editor. This step is optional, but I heartily recommend it. At a minimum, these plugins will provide syntax highlighting for CoffeeScript files, which I find very helpful. In addition, most plugins integrate with the editor to allow you to run or compile CoffeeScript snippets without leaving the editor. You don't *need* these features, but you may find them convenient.

 We'll discuss CoffeeScript support in some of the most popular editors, but there are plugins available for many more. A full list is available on the CoffeeScript wiki at `https://github.com/jashkenas/coffee-script/wiki/Text-editor-plugins/`.

Follow the instructions to install CoffeeScript in your editor of choice. After installing, restart your editor and try it out by opening `setup.coffee`. You will see some simple syntax highlighting on the code we just wrote to indicate that the plugin is working correctly.

Support in TextMate

Jeremy Ashkenas, the creator of CoffeeScript, has written a TextMate bundle that provides syntax highlighting, snippets, and inline compilation. Visit the project homepage at `https://github.com/jashkenas/coffee-script-tmbundle` and follow the installation instructions.

Support in Sublime Text 2

Sublime Text users have several choices available for CoffeeScript support.

One option is to use parts of the TextMate bundle. To use this, create a `CoffeeScript` directory in Sublime Text's `plugin` directory (on OS X, this is found at `~/Library/Application Support/Sublime Text 2`). Then, download the bundle, extract `Syntaxes/CoffeeScript.tmLanguage` and `Preferences/CoffeeScript.tmPreferences` and place these files in the new directory. To simplify the process, you can download these two files directly using the following URLs:

- `https://raw.github.com/jashkenas/coffee-script-tmbundle/master/Syntaxes/CoffeeScript.tmLanguage`
- `https://raw.github.com/jashkenas/coffee-script-tmbundle/master/Preferences/CoffeeScript.tmPreferences`

The other option is to use the native Sublime Text plugin for CoffeeScript. This offers more features and is built specifically for Sublime Text. Visit the project homepage at `http://xavura.github.io/CoffeeScript-Sublime-Plugin/` and follow the installation instructions.

Support in Vim

A Vim script is available that provides syntax highlighting as well as a `:CoffeeCompile` command to compile CoffeeScript on the fly. Visit the project homepage at `https://github.com/kchmck/vim-coffee-script/` and follow the installation instructions.

> The official repository for this plugin may be abandoned by the original maintainer, and there are several annoying bugs that have gone unfixed. You may wish to install a patched version from one of the several active forks of the project instead, such as `https://github.com/CITguy/vim-coffee-script/`. Follow the provided installation instructions, but be sure to download files from GitHub and not vim.org. Substitute the fork you are using whenever the instructions specify `kchmck/vim-coffee-script`.

Support in Emacs

There is an Emacs Major Mode named `coffee-mode` that provides syntax highlighting, menu support, and on-the-fly compiling. Install it from the Emacs package archive, or visit the project homepage at `https://github.com/defunkt/coffee-mode` for more information.

Starting our web application

Now that we know how to compile a CoffeeScript file, let's use it in a web page! We'll create a simple web page that uses CoffeeScript to read a configuration object and insert text into the page. This page will be used by the owner of a small pet shop. We'll insert the owner's name dynamically, so it can be easily changed if needed. First let's create a simple `index.html`:

```
<!DOCTYPE html>
<html>
  <head>
    <title>The Pet Shop</title>
      </head>
  <body>
    <h1>Welcome to <span id="owner_name"></span>'s Pet Shop</h1>
    <script src="setup.js"></script>
  </body>
</html>
```

You'll notice that we have a script tag pointing to our JavaScript file, just like normal. The web application doesn't need to know anything about our CoffeeScript files. It will run the compiled JavaScript output, happily ignorant of the original source.

 It *is* possible to make your browser aware of CoffeeScript, and make it run CoffeeScript code directly. However, this is an advanced technique and not really necessary to get you started, so throughout the book we will always compile to JavaScript and run that. If you'd like to learn more about this technique, see *Chapter 10, Using CoffeeScript in more places.*

Let's get rid of that annoying alert in `setup.coffee`, and update it with a configuration object and some code to insert the owner's name into the page heading. You probably know how you would write this in JavaScript. It's similar in CoffeeScript, so see if you can follow along:

```
shop = {
  owner: { name: "Ian" }
}
nameElement = document.getElementById("owner_name")
nameElement.innerHTML = shop.owner.name
```

Now we'll run the compiler again so that it updates the JavaScript. This time, we'll pass it the whole directory as an argument instead of our single file. This will compile any CoffeeScript files it finds in the directory, which will come in handy later, when we have more than one CoffeeScript file.

```
coffee -c .
```

Our `setup.js` has been updated, so load `index.html` in a web page, and it should say **Welcome to Ian's Pet Shop**.

One more thing

Let's make one small addition to our web application. We should update the title of the window with the owner's name as well. Before we edit our CoffeeScript file, it's time to learn a very helpful feature of the coffee command-line tool. Passing it the `-w` option when compiling will tell the tool to watch the source files or directory, and recompile them any time the files change. This saves you the trouble of going back to the command line and performing the compilation again every time you save a file. Start the compiler:

```
coffee -w -c .
```

 For a full reference of options available from the command line tool, visit `http://coffeescript.org/#usage` or run `coffee --help`.

Now edit `setup.coffee` to add a line at the end:

```
shop = {
  owner: { name: "Ian" }
}
nameElement = document.getElementById("owner_name")
nameElement.innerHTML = shop.owner.name
document.title = shop.owner.name + "'s Pet Shop"
```

When you save the file, `setup.js` will be updated automatically. Reload the page, and you should now see the new name in the title bar. Cool, huh?

 If you'd like to take this a step further, you could try out a tool like LiveReload. It watches your code and not only recompiles when it sees a change, but also reloads the page in your browser! Learn more at `http://livereload.com/`.

Summary

This chapter wasn't all fun and games, but it was worth it. We installed CoffeeScript and got everything configured properly. We also tried out some command-line tools to see how CoffeeScript development works, and to whet our appetites for more. We:

- Walked through the steps of installing Node.js (the platform that CoffeeScript uses to run)
- Installed CoffeeScript itself
- Tried out the CoffeeScript console, and learned to compile files with the command-line tool
- Built a very simple web page, and learned how to use the command-line tool to automatically recompile when we change our CoffeeScript files

Now we're all set up and ready to dive into the language itself, which is exactly what we'll do in the next chapter! We'll start by learning the basic syntax of CoffeeScript, and we'll get to see how it works and how it is related to JavaScript. We'll learn about variables, functions, loops, data structures, and more, and we'll get to play around with a lot of code samples. I hope you've got your command line ready!

2
Writing Your First Lines of CoffeeScript

In this chapter, we will dive into CoffeeScript headfirst. We'll look at all the simple data types and control structures, and find out how CoffeeScript helps us deal with them more simply and expressively. We'll discover some neat tricks that save us keystrokes and reduce the likelihood of errors in our code. And we'll peek under the hood to see how some of the CoffeeScript magic is happening.

In this chapter, you can expect to:

- Learn CoffeeScript syntax for many common operations
- Learn how to use standard data types and control structures in CoffeeScript
- See how the CoffeeScript we write maps back to JavaScript once compiled

Following along with the examples

I implore you to open up a console as you read this chapter and try out the examples for yourself. You don't strictly *have* to; I'll show you any important output from the example code. However, following along will make you more comfortable with the command-line tools, give you a chance to write some CoffeeScript yourself, and most importantly, will give you an opportunity to experiment. Try changing the examples in small ways to see what happens. If you're confused about a piece of code, playing around and looking at the outcome will often help you understand what's really going on.

The easiest way to follow along is to simply open up a CoffeeScript console. Remember how we did that in the previous chapter? Just run this from the command line to get an interactive console:

```
coffee
```

If you'd like to save all your code to return to later, or if you wish to work on something more complicated, you can create files instead and run those. Give your files the `.coffee` extension, and run them like this:

```
coffee my_sample_code.coffee
```

Seeing the compiled JavaScript

The golden rule of CoffeeScript, according to the CoffeeScript documentation, is:

> *It's just JavaScript.*

This means that it is a language that compiles down to JavaScript in a simple fashion, without any complicated extra moving parts. This also means that it's easy, with a little practice, to understand how the CoffeeScript you are writing will compile into JavaScript. Your JavaScript expertise is still applicable, but you are freed from the tedious parts of the language. You should understand how the generated JavaScript will work, but you do not need to actually *write* the JavaScript.

To this end, we'll spend a fair amount of time, especially in this chapter, comparing CoffeeScript code to the compiled JavaScript results. It's like peeking behind the wizard's curtain! The new language features won't seem so intimidating once you know how they work, and you'll find you have more trust in CoffeeScript when you can check in on the code it's generating. After a while, you won't even need to check in at all.

I'll show you the corresponding JavaScript for most of the examples in this chapter, but if you write your own code, you may want to examine the output. This is a great way to experiment and learn more about the language! Unfortunately, if you're using the CoffeeScript console to follow along, there isn't a great way to see the compiled output (most of the time, it's nice to have all that out of sight—just not right now!). You can see the compiled JavaScript in several other easy ways, though. The first is to put your code in a file and compile it, as we showed you above and in the previous chapter. The other is to use the **Try CoffeeScript** tool on `http://coffeescript.org/`. It brings up an editor right in the browser that updates the output as you type.

CoffeeScript basics

Let's get started! We'll begin with something simple:

```
x = 1 + 1
```

You can probably guess what JavaScript this will compile to:

```
var x;
x = 1 + 1;
```

Statements

One of the very first things you will notice about CoffeeScript is that there are no semicolons. Statements are ended by a new line. The parser usually knows if a statement should be continued on the next line. You can explicitly tell it to continue to the next line by using a backslash at the end of the first line:

```
x = 1\
  + 1
```

It's also possible to stretch function calls across multiple lines, as is common in "fluent" JavaScript interfaces:

```
"foo"
  .concat("barbaz")
  .replace("foobar", "fubar")
```

You may occasionally wish to place more than one statement on a single line (for purely stylistic purposes). This is the one time when you will use a semicolon in CoffeeScript:

```
x = 1; y = 2
```

Both of these situations are fairly rare. The vast majority of the time, you'll find that one statement per line works great. You might feel a pang of loss for your semicolons at first, but give it time. The calluses on your pinky finger will fall off, your eyes will adjust to the lack of clutter, and soon enough you won't remember what good you ever saw in semicolons.

Variables

CoffeeScript variables look a lot like JavaScript variables, with one big difference: no var! CoffeeScript puts all variables in the local scope by default.

```
x = 1
y = 2
z = x + y
```

compiles to:

```
var x, y, z;
x = 1;
y = 2;
z = x + y;
```

Believe it or not, this is one of my *absolute top favorite things* about CoffeeScript. It's so easy to accidentally introduce variables to the global scope in JavaScript and create subtle problems for yourself. You never need to worry about that again; from now on, it's handled automatically. Nothing is getting into the global scope unless you want it there.

If you *really* want to put a variable in the global scope and you're *really* sure it's a good idea, you can easily do this by attaching it to the top-level object. In the CoffeeScript console, or in Node.js programs, this is the `global` object:

```
global.myGlobalVariable = "I'm so worldly!"
```

In a browser, we use the `window` object instead:

```
window.myGlobalVariable = "I'm so worldly!"
```

Comments

Any line that begins with a # is a comment. Anything after a # in the middle of a line will also be a comment.

```
# This is a comment.
"Hello" # This is also a comment
```

Most of the time, CoffeeScripters use only this style, even for multiline comments.

```
# Most multiline comments simply wrap to the
# next line, each begun with a # and a space.
```

It is also possible (but rare in the CoffeeScript world) to use a **block comment**, which begins and ends with ###. The lines in between these characters do not need to begin with a #.

```
###
This is a block comment. You can get artistic in here.
<(^^)>
###
```

Regular comments are not included in the compiled JavaScript, but block comments are, delineated by /* */.

Calling functions

Function invocation can look very familiar in CoffeeScript:

```
console.log("Hello, planet!")
```

Other than the missing semicolon, that's exactly like JavaScript, right? But function invocation can also look different:

```
console.log "Hello, planet!"
```

Whoa! Now we're in unfamiliar ground. This will work exactly the same as the previous example, though. Any time you call a function *with arguments*, the parentheses are optional. This also works with more than one argument:

```
Math.pow 2, 3
```

While you might be a little nervous writing this way at first, I encourage you to try it and give yourself time to become comfortable with it. Idiomatic CoffeeScript style eliminates parentheses whenever it's sensible to do so. What do I mean by "sensible"? Well, imagine you're reading your code for the first time, and ask yourself which style makes it easiest to comprehend. Usually it's most readable without parentheses, but there are some occasions when your code is complex enough that judicious use of parentheses will help. Use your best judgment, and everything will turn out fine.

There is one exception to the optional parentheses rule. If you are invoking a function *with no arguments,* you must use parentheses:

```
Date.now()
```

Why? The reason is simple. CoffeeScript preserves JavaScript's treatment of functions as **first-class citizens**.

```
myFunc = Date.now
  #=> myFunc holds a function object that hasn't been executed
myDate = Date.now()
  #=> myDate holds the result of the function's execution
```

CoffeeScript's syntax is looser, but it must still be unambiguous. When no arguments are present, it's not clear whether you want to access the function object or execute the function. Requiring parentheses makes it clear which one you want, and still allows both kinds of functionality. This is part of CoffeeScript's philosophy of not deviating from the fundamentals of the JavaScript language. If functions were always executed instead of returned, CoffeeScript would no longer act like JavaScript, and it would be hard for you, the seasoned JavaScripter, to know what to expect. This way, once you understand a few simple concepts, you will know exactly what your code is doing.

From this discussion, we can extract a more general principle: *parentheses are optional, except when necessary to avoid ambiguity*. Here's another situation in which you might encounter ambiguity: nested function calls.

```
Math.max 2, 3, Math.min 4, 5, 6
```

Yikes! What's happening there? Well, you can easily clear this up by adding parentheses. You may add parentheses to all the function calls, or you may add just enough to resolve the ambiguity:

```
# These two calls are equivalent
Math.max(2, 3, Math.min(4, 5, 6))
Math.max 2, 3, Math.min(4, 5, 6)
```

This makes it clear that you wish `min` to take 4 and 5 as arguments. If you wished 6 to be an argument to `max` instead, you would place the parentheses differently.

```
# These two calls are equivalent
Math.max(2, 3, Math.min(4, 5), 6)
Math.max 2, 3, Math.min(4, 5), 6
```

Precedence

Actually, the original version I showed you is valid CoffeeScript too! You just need to understand the precedence rules that CoffeeScript uses for functions. Arguments are assigned to functions from the *inside out*. Another way to think of this is that an argument belongs to the function that it's *nearest* to. So our original example is equivalent to the first variation we used, in which 4, 5, and 6 are arguments to `min`:

```
# These two calls are equivalent
Math.max 2, 3, Math.min 4, 5, 6
Math.max 2, 3, Math.min(4, 5, 6)
```

The parentheses are only absolutely necessary if our desired behavior doesn't match CoffeeScript's precedence — in this case, if we wanted 6 to be a argument to `max`. This applies to an unlimited level of nesting:

```
threeSquared = Math.pow 3, Math.floor Math.min 4, Math.sqrt 5
```

Of course, at some point the elimination of parentheses turns from the question of if you *can* to if you *should*. You are now a master of the intricacies of CoffeeScript function-call parsing, but the other programmers reading your code might not be (and even if they are, they might prefer not to puzzle out what your code is doing). Avoid parentheses in simple cases, and use them judiciously in the more complicated situations.

Control structures

Control structures (such as if, else, and so on) in CoffeeScript share a foundation with JavaScript. We'll start out with some constructions that will feel familiar except some slightly different syntax. However, we'll then build on those basics and explore some new ways to express control flow.

So far, most of the CoffeeScript syntax we have covered has been somewhat superficial. Less punctuation makes code more readable (and prettier!), but CoffeeScript promises more than that. As we work through these control structures, you'll get a taste of some improvements that make CoffeeScript a more expressive language. Code isn't just machine instructions, it's also a form of communication. Good code not only works as intended, but communicates to other humans about what it is doing and how it is doing that. In this section we'll see some ways that CoffeeScript helps you communicate more effectively.

Using if statements

The first structure we'll look at is the standard if statement. Let's start off with a simple construction:

```
if (true == true)
  console.log "Tautology!"
```

If you're trying out these examples in the CoffeeScript console, you'll need to enter **multiline mode** to do so – otherwise the console will try to execute the first line before you have a chance to enter the rest! Hit *Ctrl-V* on the first line of your statement to change to multiline mode. The prompt will change from **coffee>** to **------>** to indicate that you've changed mode. Remember to enter the indentation for each line in the console, it's important! Here's what this statement will look like in the console:

```
------> if (true == true)
.......     "f"
```

When you're finished, hit *Enter* to create a blank line, then hit *Ctrl-V* again to exit multiline mode. The console will now evaluate your statement and return a result.

If you've been following along with the other sections, you probably won't be surprised to hear that it's possible (and common) to eliminate the parentheses in the test statement:

```
if true == true
  console.log "Tautology!"
```

You've probably noticed another omission by now: curly braces. CoffeeScript doesn't use curly braces for any code control structures like ifs, loops, or functions. Instead, it uses indentation to control code execution. Code that goes inside the `if` statement is indented beyond the level of the `if` statement. When CoffeeScript reaches a non-empty line that isn't indented to that level, it knows it has reached the end of the statement.

The idea of using whitespace semantically is born out of the observation that almost all languages encourage programmers to indent code for the sake of readability. In most languages, the whitespace is ignored by the machine, but it's expected by your fellow humans. Using whitespace semantically simply makes it important to both the machine and humans. Once the whitespace can convey instructions to the machine, other pieces of syntax become irrelevant and can be removed (in this case, curly braces).

Many programmers have trouble coming to terms with the idea of semantic whitespace. Python, as the most prominent language to use it, has taken a lot of flak for the choice. There are a few valid technical criticisms leveled against semantic whitespace (most notably that it is troublesome when cut-and-pasting code), but like many other hotly-debated issues, it generally comes down to a matter of taste.

If you're one of those people who feel squeamish about semantic whitespace, let me offer this comfort: I was (and occasionally still am) one of those people too. Even though I love CoffeeScript, I've never been completely sold on the whitespace. The good news is that it impacts your daily coding much less than you might expect. Whether or not you like the theory, in practice the whitespace issues will quickly fade into the background, and only rarely will you notice them at all. You'll come to appreciate the many other expressive features of the language, but you'll probably never think about the whitespace again as much as you have right now.

If you nest statements, you simply nest indentation levels as needed. CoffeeScript will know how to handle the successive levels of indentation.

```
number = 6
console.log "Let's test our number."
if number > 5
  console.log "Our number is greater than 5"
  if number > 10
    console.log "Our number is greater than 10"
  console.log "Now we're done testing."
```

Our CoffeeScript whitespace is transformed into the proper curly braces in JavaScript. Notice the correct nesting of `if` statements.

```javascript
var number;
number = 6;
console.log("Let's test our number.");
if (number > 5) {
  console.log("Our number is greater than 5");
  if (number > 10) {
    console.log("Our number is greater than 10");
  }
  console.log("Now we're done testing.");
}
```

The else and else if statements

You might be able to guess that `else` and `else if` statements are also available. They work much the same as in JavaScript, though again without the need for curly braces, and parentheses are optional.

```coffeescript
number = -8
if number > 0
  "Positive"
else if number < 0
  "Negative"
else
  "Zero"
```

The unless statement

Now let's look at something that doesn't have an exact equivalent in JavaScript. The `unless` statement behaves much like an `if`, but it executes the block if its test returns a **false-ish** value instead of a **true-ish** value.

```coffeescript
day = "Monday"
unless day[0] == "S"
  console.log "This is a weekday."
```

This can replace the common `if (!test)` form found in JavaScript. In fact, that is exactly what an `unless` block compiles to:

```javascript
var day;
day = "Monday";
if (day[0] !== "S") {
  console.log("This is a weekday.");
}
```

Using `unless` helps your code read more like spoken language – instead of reading as "if not this condition holds", it reads as "unless this condition holds". Using `unless` can also reduce errors. When reading code, it's easy to overlook a ! character and think that a whole block does the opposite of what it actually does. An `unless` keyword is much more obvious.

You can also use `else` and `else if` in combination with `unless`.

```
day = "Monday"
unless day[0] == "S"
  console.log "This is a weekday."
else
  console.log "It's the weekend!"
```

Be careful, though! It's easy to write confusing statements if you take this too far. Once you start adding alternatives, stop and ask yourself if you should refactor your code into something simpler (at this point, a standard `if` often makes the most sense).

Single-line form

A common pattern in code is the need to execute a single line if a condition holds. JavaScripters have developed a number of ways to handle that situation, like this:

```
if (true === true) {
  console.log("Truth achieved!");
}
```

Or this:

```
if (true === true) { console.log("Truth achieved!"); }
```

Or this (my personal least favorite):

```
if (true === true)
  console.log("Truth achieved!");
```

CoffeeScript has a simple way to deal with this pattern that is less error-prone and more readable. Simply put the `if` clause *after* the code to execute:

```
console.log "Truth achieved!" if true == true
```

This compiles into the first JavaScript form I showed you. See how the CoffeeScript version reads well as human language? "Do an action if these conditions are met." You can also use `unless` in this form, and it reads equally well.

```
console.log "Universe error!" unless true == true
```

Comparison operators

Now that we know how to use these control structures, let's learn about some comparison operators we can use to test the truthfulness of useful questions. There's one big surprise in here, so let's get that out of the way. `==` and `!=` in CoffeeScript don't compile to their equivalents in JavaScript.

```
1 == 2
3 != 4
```

becomes:

```
1 === 2;
3 !== 4;
```

> According to the CoffeeScript documentation, this decision was made because "the `==` operator frequently causes undesirable coercion, is intransitive, and has a different meaning than in other languages".
>
> Most JavaScripters recommend using `===` and `!==` exclusively, so this is simply enshrining that best practice. If you wish to know more about this recommendation, read `http://www.impressivewebs.com/why-use-triple-equals-javascipt/`.

Other than that surprise, the other common JavaScript operators are all present and work as you might expect.

```
if 1 < 2 && 3 >= 2
  if false || true
    if !false
      console.log "All is well."
```

However, CoffeeScript also provides a number of aliases to improve your code's readability. You can use `is` and `isnt` to test equality:

```
status = "normal"
reactor = "primed"
console.log "All clear" if status is "normal"
console.log "Abort mission" if reactor isnt "primed"
```

These aliases compile down to the ordinary JavaScript forms:

```
status = "normal";
reactor = "primed";
if (status === "normal") {
  console.log("All clear");
}
```

```
if (reactor !== "primed") {
  console.log("Abort mission");
}
```

You can use and, or, and not to combine truth values:

```
location = "Washington"
hairy = false
blurryPhoto = true
manInApeSuit = false
isBigfoot = location is "Washington" and (hairy or blurryPhoto)\
  and not manInApeSuit
```

These too become the normal forms in JavaScript:

```
isBigfoot = location === "Washington" && (hairy || blurryPhoto)
  && !manInApeSuit;
```

 In some languages, such as PHP and Ruby, the and keyword actually behaves differently than &&. In those languages there are subtle precedence differences between the two. Don't worry! That's not the case in CoffeeScript, since they both compile to the same result in JavaScript.

Even true and false have aliases. true can be written as yes or on, and false can be no or off. Use of these aliases is entirely optional, but you may find that a certain version is the most readable in any given situation.

```
power = true
mute = false
if power is on
  playingMusic = yes if mute is off
else
  playingMusic = no
```

Here's the JavaScript. Notice that using these aliases with is means we are strictly comparing against the boolean values, which is a little different than only testing the **truthiness**.

```
if (power === true) {
  if (mute === false) {
    playingMusic = true;
  }
} else {
  playingMusic = false;
}
```

Here's the whole table of comparison operators, from the CoffeeScript documentation. We'll look at in and of in the next two sections, when we deal with arrays and objects, respectively.

CoffeeScript	JavaScript
is	===
isnt	!==
not	!
and	&&
or	||
true, yes, on	true
false, no, off	false
@, this	this
of	in
in	no JS equivalent

Arrays

Arrays, at their most simple, look very similar to JavaScript.

```
languages = [ "english", "spanish", "french" ]
console.log languages[1]
```

You may use a trailing comma and it will be compiled away:

```
languages = [
  "english",
  "spanish",
  "french",
]
```

becomes:

```
var languages;
languages = ["english", "spanish", "french"];
```

Many people prefer this style, as it makes it easier to change the contents of an array or object. And you'll be thankful for this safeguard if you've ever left a trailing comma in a JavaScript array, only to discover (always at a very inconvenient time) that it causes an execution-halting error in one particular browser. The browser in question will remain unnamed for the sake of our collective blood pressure. I want this book to be a book about *nice* things. *Happy* things.

If you're feeling daring, you can eschew commas altogether. That's right! When the members of your array are declared on separate lines, you may omit the commas and CoffeeScript will still know what to do.

```
languages = [
  "english"
  "spanish"
  "french"
]
```

Ranges

Sometimes, when declaring an array, you wish to initialize it with a simple range of values. It's tiresome to write out the values by hand, and difficult to check for errors once you're done. Luckily, there's a better way!

```
singleDigits = [0..9]
```

This compiles into a normal JavaScript array containing all elements in the range you specified.

```
var singleDigits;
singleDigits = [0, 1, 2, 3, 4, 5, 6, 7, 8, 9];
```

You can use descending order as well:

```
countdown = [10..1]
```

Two dots makes the range **inclusive** (meaning it will include the ending number you give it), while three dots make it **exclusive** (meaning it won't).

```
[1..5]  == [1, 2, 3, 4, 5]
[1...5] == [1, 2, 3, 4]
```

You can even create a range using variables instead of literal numbers.

```
start = 0
end = 1000
bigNumbers = [start..end]
```

The generated JavaScript gets a little more complicated when the range uses anything other than number literals. If you want a quick brain teaser, check it out for yourself and see if you can decipher what it's doing.

```
var end, start, _i, _results;
start = 0;
end = 1000;

bigNumbers = (function() {
  _results = [];
  for (var _i = start;
    start <= end ? _i <= end : _i >= end;
    start <= end ? _i++ : _i--)
  { _results.push(_i); }
  return _results;
}).apply(this);
```

Loops

Iterating through the elements of an array has always been a bit of a sore point in JavaScript. The `for` loop is tried and true, but writing it out every time is a lot of unnecessary keystrokes, and makes your code more verbose. There's the functional-style `Array.prototype.forEach`, which works well but isn't supported in every browser (I think we all know who the culprit is). And some libraries, such as jQuery or Underscore.js, provide their own iteration utilities, but of course those are only available if you have the library loaded up. What to do? Why, use CoffeeScript, of course!

```
animals = ["dog", "cat", "bird"]
for animal in animals
  console.log animal
```

As usual, the generated JavaScript looks very much like something you or I might write:

```
var animal, animals, _i, _len;
animals = ["dog", "cat", "bird"];
for (_i = 0, _len = animals.length; _i < _len; _i++) {
  animal = animals[_i];
  console.log(animal);
}
```

If the body of our loop only contains one statement, we can declare the whole thing on a single line, with the `for` at the end (just like we could do with `if` and `unless` earlier). The example above could be rewritten like this:

```
animals = ["dog", "cat", "bird"]
console.log animal for animal in animals
```

One extremely useful feature of CoffeeScript loops is that they return a value—an array of the results of the inner statement for every item in the loop. If you've ever used `Array.prototype.map` to transform an array, you'll be happy to see that it's easy to achieve the same functionality in CoffeeScript.

```
animals = ["dog", "cat", "bird"]
pluralAnimals = for animal in animals
  animal + "s"
```

If we look at the compiled JavaScript, we can see that it's still using a `for` loop. It's just doing an extra bit of work to push the results into an array that's returned at the end:

```
var animal, animals, pluralAnimals;
animals = ["dog", "cat", "bird"];
pluralAnimals = (function() {
  var _i, _len, _results;
  _results = [];
  for (_i = 0, _len = animals.length; _i < _len; _i++) {
    animal = animals[_i];
    _results.push(animal + "s");
  }
  return _results;
})();
```

We can also shorten our operation to a single line. There's one catch to be aware of, though. What do you notice about the following code?

```
animals = ["dog", "cat", "bird"]
pluralAnimals = (animal + "s" for animal in animals)
console.log pluralAnimals
```

After we've spent all this time cutting out unneeded parentheses, it seems strange that I'm adding a set around this statement. As it turns out, they are needed. To see why, you'll need to understand how CoffeeScript handles precedence with assignment and loops. What if we wrote it without the parentheses, like this?

```
pluralAnimals = animal + "s" for animal in animals
```

The assignment has a higher precedence, so that version works out like this:

```
(pluralAnimals = animal + "s") for animal in animals
```

The assignment takes place *inside* the loop for each member of the array, so when we examine `pluralAnimals` at the end, we'll find it holds the value of the last transformed element, in this case, `"birds"`. This usually isn't what we want, so we put parentheses around the for loop. This ensures that the result of the entire loop is what's assigned to our variable.

Loop comprehensions

Iterating through an array is nice, but it's time to get fancier. We'll often find that we want to loop through an array, but only act on elements which meet a certain criteria. We can do this by putting `if` statements inside our loop, but there's a much better way. CoffeeScript lets us attach **guards**—conditional statements that filter the loop execution—using the `when` keyword.

```
words = ["dogma", "catastrophe", "doggerel", "hangdog"]
for word in words when word.indexOf("dog") isnt -1
  console.log word
```

Sure enough, when compiled to JavaScript, the guard appears as an `if` statement inside the loop.

```
var word, words, _i, _len;
words = ["dogma", "catastrophe", "doggerel", "hangdog"];
for (_i = 0, _len = words.length; _i < _len; _i++) {
  word = words[_i];
  if (word.indexOf("dog") !== -1) {
    console.log(word);
  }
}
```

Let's combine a few of the array tricks we've learned. We can assign the result of a loop with guards to a variable, and it will store an array of only the values that met the criteria. And remember how ranges helped us easily build arrays of sequential numbers? Turns out ranges are very useful when combined with loops.

```
evenNumbers = (n + " is even" for n in [1..100] when n % 2 is 0)
```

There's a lot happening on that line, but it's not so bad once we break it apart. We start with an array of the numbers from 1 to `100`. We iterate through the array, only operating on numbers that are divisible by 2. For every number that fits this criteria, we turn it into a string. Our `evenNumbers` variable is then assigned to hold the array of resulting strings.

A few more array tricks

There's even more that we can do with loop comprehensions in CoffeeScript, although we'll use these features less frequently.

Occasionally we'll want to iterate through an array, but we'll need access to the index of the element we're currently working with. In these situations, `for` can take a second argument that holds the current index.

```
solarSystem = [
  "Mercury"
  "Venus"
  "Earth"
  "Mars"
  "Jupiter"
  "Saturn"
  "Uranus"
  "Neptune"
  "Pluto"
]
for planet, planetIndex in solarSystem when planet isnt "Pluto"
  console.log "Planet #" + (planetIndex+1) + " is " + planet
```

We may also have an occasional need to iterate through every **nth** member of an array — every second item, or every fifth item, or whatever the situation calls for. CoffeeScript makes this easy with the `by` keyword. We can rewrite our even-number example using this instead of the modulo operator. Only we'll need to start at 2, because `by` starts counting with the first item of the array.

```
evenNumbers = (n for n in [2..100] by 2)
```

Checking array membership

We've used the `in` keyword while iterating through arrays, but it serves double duty. We can also use it to check for membership in an array.

```
number = 3
if number in [2, 3, 5, 7, 11, 13]
  console.log number + " is prime!"
```

The compiled JavaScript for this is very straightforward. Because CoffeeScript has access to the array, it simply splits the values out into different equality tests.

```
var number;
number = 3;
```

```
if (number === 2 || number === 3 || number === 5 || number === 7 ||
number === 11 || number === 13) {
  console.log(number + " is prime!");
}
```

We can also use `in` for more advanced situations, such as when the array is dynamic.

```
planets = [ "Mercury", "Venus", "Earth", "Mars",
            "Jupiter", "Saturn", "Uranus", "Neptune", ]
console.log "Hooray!" if "Pluto" in planets
```

The compiled JavaScript for this situation behaves the same way, but by necessity is somewhat more complex:

```
var planets,
  __indexOf = [].indexOf || function(item) {
    for (var i = 0, l = this.length; i < l; i++) {
      if (i in this && this[i] === item) return i;
    }
    return -1;
  };

planets = ["Mercury", "Venus", "Earth", "Mars", "Jupiter", "Saturn",
"Uranus", "Neptune"];
if (__indexOf.call(planets, "Pluto") >= 0) {
  console.log("Hooray!");
}
```

 You can see that CoffeeScript has defined a small utility function in this example, named __indexOf. Several of these helper functions will appear over time. They allow CoffeeScript to generate code that is compatible with every JavaScript runtime and doesn't rely on any external libraries. These helpers are kept small and efficient, and luckily CoffeeScript is smart enough to only generate them once per file.

Simple objects

You have no doubt spent a lot of time working with objects in JavaScript. They are the most versatile data structure in the language, and JavaScript encourages heavy use of them. CoffeeScript keeps all that great support for objects, and adds a few helpful features for dealing with them.

Declaring an object looks very familiar. Let's record a few biographical details:

```
author = { name: "Ian", age: 26 }
```

We can still access object properties like we do in JavaScript:

```
author.name
author["age"]
author.favoriteLanguage = "CoffeeScript"
```

Just like CoffeeScript arrays, if we declare the object properties on different lines, we can optionally omit the commas.

```
authorsBicycle = {
  color: "black"
  fenders: true
  gears: 24
}
```

That's not all! We can also omit the curly braces. This is possible on both the single-line and multi-line versions.

```
author = name: "Ian", age: 26, favoriteLanguage: "CoffeeScript"
authorsBicycle =
  color: "black"
  fenders: true
  gears: 24
```

This even works with nested objects. If we omit the curly braces, CoffeeScript uses the indentation to determine the structure of the object.

```
authorsBicycle =
  color: "black"
  brand:
    make: "Surly"
    model: "Cross Check"
  fenders: true
  gears: 24
```

This compiles to a nested object:

```
var authorsBike;
authorsBike = {
  color: "black",
  brand: {
    make: "Surly",
    model: "Cross Check"
```

```
  },
  fenders: true,
  gears: 24
};
```

Iterating over objects

Happily, CoffeeScript also makes it easy to iterate over the properties of an object. Remember, we iterated over arrays using `for item in array`. Objects have a very similar syntax, but use the `of` keyword instead of `in`. This can be a little confusing if you think back to the `in` keyword in JavaScript, so try to put that out of your mind. I remember the difference by thinking of describing it in English: you have items *in* an array, but you have properties *of* an object. The loop takes two values, the **key** and **value** of the property.

```
author = name: "Ian", age: 26, favoriteLanguage: "CoffeeScript"
for k, v of author
  console.log "My " + k + " is " + v
```

The compiled JavaScript is again a very simple implementation, using the `in` JavaScript keyword (which we're still not thinking too hard about lest we get confused again).

```
for (k in author) {
  v = author[k];
  console.log("My " + k + " is " + v);
}
```

Summary

We've covered a lot of ground in this chapter. We learned:

- How to use variables.

- How to call functions.

- How to use `if/else` statements and their counterpart, `unless`.

- How to use natural-language aliases to make our comparison statements more readable.

- How to declare arrays, and iterate through their contents in a number of different ways.

- How to declare and iterate over objects.

Not only did we learn about all those things, but we made sure to avoid a few common mistakes, and learned why it was possible to make those mistakes. We've compared many of the CoffeeScript statements to the compiled JavaScript, so hopefully you're developing a good mental map of how CoffeeScript translates to JavaScript.

Now that we've got a solid handle on the basics, we're ready to start building our application. In the next chapter, we'll begin development of a small web application to help manage a pet shop. We'll need all of the skills we learned in this chapter, and we'll be learning a few more as we work!

Building a Simple Application

3

We've set up our CoffeeScript work environment, and we've also learned a whole bunch of new syntax for writing good CoffeeScript. Now it's time to put all of that knowledge to work! In this chapter, we'll dive into building our web application. We'll need everything we have learned in the previous chapters, but now, we'll be using it to build a cohesive product. We'll also stop along the way to learn about several more vital features of CoffeeScript that will help us build a better application.

We're going to create a web application for a small pet shop. We'll start out by creating a page to display the pets who are currently staying at the pet shop, so that prospective customers can browse and check if the shop has a pet they like. Our application will be a lightweight web page with most of the logic in JavaScript. Of course, we won't be *writing* JavaScript; we'll write CoffeeScript and let the compiler take care of the dirty work!

We will:

- Set up our web application and use it to display a list of pets
- Learn how to define functions in CoffeeScript, and how functions behave differently than they do in JavaScript
- Add dynamic behavior when a customer clicks on a pet for more information
- Learn about a new control structure
- Dynamically generate some values from our existing data and use them in our list of pets

Building our application

In *Chapter 1, Running a CoffeeScript Program*, we tested our CoffeeScript compiler by creating a bare-bones web page for a small pet shop. It's time to revisit that code, but we're more ambitious now. The first thing we need to do is use the page to display a list of available pets. Here's our `index.html`:

```html
<!DOCTYPE html>
<html>
  <head>
  <meta charset="UTF-8">
    <title>The Pet Shop</title>
    <link href="style.css" media="screen" rel="style sheet"
type="text/css" />
  </head>
  <body>
    <h1>Welcome to <span id="owner_name"></span>'s Pet Shop</h1>

    <p>We have some lovely pets available for the
    right owner to take home today. Please have a
    look at our selection.</p>

    <ul id="available_pets">
    </ul>

    <script src="setup.js"></script>
  </body>
</html>
```

It's much the same as our original version, but we've linked the code to a style sheet, added a paragraph of text welcoming visitors to the site, and created an empty list element. This will hold the list of pets currently available in the shop.

Let's add a CSS style sheet too. This isn't strictly necessary—the application will still work fine without it. But I find it much more enjoyable to work with an aesthetically pleasing application, and it helps to shape the features I add, since I can better visualize the final product. Put the following rules in `style.css`:

```css
body {
  font-family: Garamond, "Hoefler Text", "Times New Roman", Times,
serif;
  padding: 0;
  margin: 0;
  background: #FFFDF4;
}
h1 {
  font-family: Futura, "Century Gothic", AppleGothic, sans-serif;
  margin: 0;
```

```css
    padding: 0.5em;
    background: #0F7200;
    color: white;
}
body > p {
    padding: 1em;
    font-size: 1.2em;
    font-style: italic;
}
```

 You can download the code for this chapter (and all other chapters) if you'd rather not type it in by hand. Visit `http://www.packtpub.com/support` and choose **CoffeeScript Application Development** from the dropdown.

At the bottom of the page is the reference to `setup.js`, the compiled output from our CoffeeScript code. Let's work on the source file, `setup.coffee`.

 While you work on your CoffeeScript files, you will frequently want to look at the changes you make in a browser. You can manually run the command to compile your `.coffee` files every time you want to try out your changes, but this gets tiresome. A much easier method is to use the `-w` flag to the command-line tool that we learned about in *Chapter 1, Running a CoffeeScript Program*. Leave this command running in a terminal in the background, and it will automatically recompile your CoffeeScript every time you save a file. From the directory containing your `.coffee` files, run this:

```
coffee -c -w
```

First, we'll declare an object that holds the data for our shop. Eventually, this data might come from a database or other external source, but since right now our pet shop is small and doesn't need to handle many pets, we'll use simple objects and keep the data right inside our code:

```coffeescript
shop = {
    owner: { name: "Ian" }
    animals: [
        { name: "Kelsey", type: "dog" }
        { name: "Sgt. Snuffles", type: "dog" }
        { name: "Chomps", type: "rabbit" }
        { name: "Flops", type: "rabbit" }
        { name: "Bopper", type: "rabbit" }
        { name: "Chairman Meow", type: "cat" }
        { name: "Jacques", type: "cat" }
```

```
        { name: "Chupa", type: "cat" }
        { name: "Alfred", type: "horse" }
    ]
}
```

This object contains the owner information, as it did before, but now it also contains the `animals` property. This holds an array of all the current animals, stored as objects so we can record additional information about them.

Next, we'll repeat the page initialization that we performed in *Chapter 1, Running a CoffeeScript Program*. This pulls information about the owner from the `store` object and adds it to the page content.

```
nameElement = document.getElementById("owner_name")
nameElement.innerHTML = shop.owner.name
document.title = shop.owner.name + "'s Pet Shop"
```

You might have noticed that we're interacting with the DOM here, using familiar functions and properties such as `document.getElementById` and `innerHTML`. This is one of the beautiful things about CoffeeScript's close relationship with JavaScript. Everything that is available to JavaScript is also available to CoffeeScript, and can be called without doing any extra work. Likewise, if you want to use external JavaScript libraries (such as jQuery or Backbone.js) they are fully available to, and callable from, your CoffeeScript code.

Throughout this book, the example code will be designed to work with *modern* web browsers. In a production application, we would need to to take a number of extra steps to ensure that our application worked well across older browsers. However, it's a better learning experience if we don't get bogged down in the minutiae of cross-browser compatibility and make use of some advanced features. At times, we will make judicious use of new JavaScript APIs, HTML5 elements, and CSS3 features. For this reason, I highly recommend following along on a capable browser. If you are using Internet Explorer, use version 9 or higher. For most other browsers, any recent version will work wonderfully.

Finally, let's display that list of animals on our page! Our HTML already contains an empty list, so we just need to build some content and insert it into that element.

```
petOutput = for pet in shop.animals
  "<li>" + pet.name + "</li>"

availablePets = document.getElementById("available_pets")
availablePets.innerHTML = petOutput.join ""
```

For each pet, we create a list element containing the pet's name. We store the result of the loop as `petOutput`. This variable will contain an array of the list element strings, such as:

```
["<li>Kelsey</li>", "<li>Sgt. Snuffles</li>", … ]
```

Once finished, we find the list element in the page and insert our generated HTML. We call `join` with an empty string to easily concatenate all the contents of the `petOutput` array.

You might wonder why I chose to build the list using an array instead of concatenating one big string like this:

```
petOutput = ""
for pet in shop.animals
    petOutput += "<li>" + pet.name + "</li>"
```

It's not a big deal when working with small arrays, but as your array grows larger you want to to avoid concatenating strings with each iteration. Strings are immutable in JavaScript, so concatenation involves creating a new string and copying the contents of the old ones into it. When this happens many times in a loop, performance suffers pretty badly. Using an array, like I did, avoids all the copying and garbage collection, and forms a large string just once, at the end. Luckily, CoffeeScript's loop constructs make it very easy for us to follow this pattern.

If everything works, you should see a page like the following screenshot:

Welcome to Ian's Pet Shop

We have some lovely pets available for the right owner to take home today. Please have a look at our selection.

- Kelsey
- Sgt. Snuffles
- Chomps
- Flops
- Bopper
- Chairman Meow
- Jacques
- Chupa
- Alfred

This is a pretty good start! Before we continue adding functionality, let's take a moment to make our code a little neater. To do this, we'll learn about a new feature of CoffeeScript: string interpolation.

String Interpolation

Anyone who writes a lot of JavaScript is very familiar with the way of building strings.

```
var verb = "mash";
var operators = "plus symbols";
"You " + verb + " them " together using " + operators + "."
```

This style leaves a little to be desired. One flaw is that it overloads the + operator, and leads to subtle bugs when combining strings and integers. It's easy to overlook the fact that 1 + 2 + "3" will behave differently than "3" + 2 + 1. The other flaw with building strings in JavaScript is that it quickly becomes difficult to read. You find yourself spending time corralling spaces and quote marks just to make sure your string turns out like you are expecting. It's especially painful anytime you find yourself constructing HTML strings by hand and wish to insert dynamic attributes. Let's not even mention the trouble you can get into mixing ' and " characters!

Thankfully, CoffeeScript has a better solution for building strings. Use #{} inside a double-quoted string to surround a dynamic value that will be inserted into the string:

```
verb = "build"
operators = "bracket enclosures"
"You #{verb} strings using #{operators}."
```

You can put any code inside the brackets; the code will be executed and the result inserted into the string:

```
"#{1 + 1}'s company, #{1 + 2} is a crowd"
"A googol is a large number: #{Math.pow 10, 100}"
```

It can even handle nested double quote characters!

```
"No problems #{"here".toUpperCase()}!"
```

Let's see what these strings look like when compiled into JavaScript:

```
"" + (1 + 1) + "'s company, " + (1 + 2) + " is a crowd";
"A googol is a large number: " + (Math.pow(10, 100));
"No problems " + ("here".toUpperCase()) + "!";
```

The strings have been converted to use +, just like we would have done if we were writing the JavaScript by hand. You can see that the CoffeeScript is very careful to preserve the correct order of operations, and makes sure that everything is cast to a string. The CoffeeScript version is a lot more pleasant to read though, don't you think?

Using string interpolation in our application

Now that we know about string interpolation, let's use it to clean up our code! We've got a couple of places where we can use this new syntax to make our strings more readable. The first is in the page initialization, where we add the owner's name to the title:

```
document.title = shop.owner.name + "'s Pet Shop"
```

Let's use interpolation here:

```
document.title = "#{shop.owner.name}'s Pet Shop"
```

That's a bit nicer. Now let's look at the second string we can clean up, in the loop to create the pet list:

```
petOutput = for pet in shop.animals
  "<li>" + pet.name + "</li>"
```

We can adjust this too:

```
petOutput = for pet in shop.animals
  "<li>#{pet.name}</li>"
```

Perfect! It's a small thing, but changes like this will keep us working quickly, long into the future. We won't spend as much time trying to figure out what the old code is doing, and when we make changes to these lines later, we won't be as likely to waste time on errors caused by missing quote marks and such.

Now that we've polished up our code a little bit, it's time to add some dynamic behavior to our application. After all, what good is our client-side code unless our application responds to user input? Before we get started adding more features, we'll take a detour to learn about one of the most important CoffeeScript fundamentals: functions.

Defining functions

Function syntax might be the single most-talked-about feature of CoffeeScript. It's notable because it is strange: it doesn't feel familiar to a programmer coming from JavaScript (or from most other languages, for that matter). You might not like it immediately, but give it some time and you'll find it grows on you. Like a foreign language, at first you may need to pause and translate the syntax back into a familiar form. Give your brain a little time to rewire, though, and soon you'll be able to read and understand CoffeeScript instantly.

Let's look at the following example:

```
(name) ->
  return "Hello, #{name}!"
```

This is a simple anonymous function that takes one argument, `name`, and returns a message saying `hello`. If you're puzzled, let's take a look at the resulting JavaScript:

```
(function(name) {
  return "Hello, " + name + "!";
});
```

The arguments declaration remains the same. JavaScript's `function` keyword and curly brace are replaced by a `->`. Just like the `if` statements we saw in *Chapter 2, Writing Your First Lines of Coffeescript*, function definitions use **semantic whitespace**. The body of the function is indented (traditionally by two spaces). The function ends at the first non-empty line that isn't indented deeper than the line that declares the function.

But wait, how do we call this function? Well, we need a way to reference it:

```
sayHello = (name) ->
  return "Hello, #{name}!"
sayHello "Ian"
```

We've assigned our function to the `sayHello` variable, and can now invoke it as we please. You'll recognize this if you've ever passed around an anonymous function in JavaScript:

```
var sayHello = function(name) {
  return "Hello, " + name + "!";
};
sayHello("Ian");
```

Functions can take multiple arguments, of course:

```
sayHelloFormally = (honorific, name) ->
  return "Good day to you, #{honorific} #{name}"
```

Functions can also take no arguments. In this case, you may omit the parentheses and use only the `->` as the function declaration:

```
sayGoodbye = ->
  return "Bye now!"
```

Function naming

Why are we assigning our function to a variable? Why not make it a named function, like we could do in JavaScript?

```
function sayHello(name) { … }
```

CoffeeScript actually doesn't support named functions in most cases. The primary reason for excluding them is that Internet Explorer treats named functions very poorly.

 You can find more information on the history of this feature on the CoffeeScript FAQ: `https://github.com/jashkenas/coffee-script/wiki/FAQ`. You can also find a long, detailed explanation of the problems with named functions at `http://kangax.github.com/nfe/`.

Luckily, assigning a variable to name a function works just as well for almost every common task in JavaScript (the one shortcoming is that debuggers will provide slightly worse stack traces). Using anonymous functions assigned to variables is predictable and simple, especially in CoffeeScript.

If you are in the habit of declaring your functions at the bottom of your JavaScript files, you will find that this no longer works. Top-level function declarations are executed before everything else in the file due to some special treatment by the language specification, but the same rules do not apply to functions assigned to variables. You have three possible solutions to this problem:

- Move your function declarations to the beginning of the file.
- Move your function declarations to a separate file that is executed first. Don't forget to put your functions in the global scope by assigning them to the `window` object.
- Put the rest of your code inside a function body, and invoke that at the end of your script.

Function return behavior

Now we're going to learn about a feature of CoffeeScript that might surprise you, but is very useful. Here's a CoffeeScript function:

```
shout = (phrase) ->
  "#{phrase.toUpperCase()}!!!"
```

Do you see anything unusual in the compiled JavaScript?

```
var shout;
shout = function (phrase) {
  return "" + (phrase.toUpperCase()) + "!!!";
}
```

The JavaScript function is returning the string, even though our CoffeeScript function never used `return`! CoffeeScript uses **implicit** returns; if it's not given an **explicit** return value, a function will return the results of the last statement it runs. CoffeeScript takes care of all the work to translate these implicit returns into explicit `return` statements in JavaScript. The following code:

```
letMeGoogolThatForYou = (number) ->
  googol = Math.pow 10, 100
  number * googol
```

Becomes:

```
letMeGoogolThatForYou = function(number) {
  var googol;
  googol = Math.pow(10, 100);
  return number * googol;
};
```

This works with control structures like `if`. Thus, the following piece of code:

```
opinion = (numberOfStars) ->
  if numberOfStars >= 4
    "Happy"
  else if numberOfStars <= 2
    "Sad"
  else
    "Neutral"
```

Becomes:

```
opinion = function(numberOfStars) {
  if (numberOfStars >= 4) {
    return "Happy";
```

```
    } else if (numberOfStars <= 2) {
      return "Sad";
    } else {
      return "Neutral";
    }
};
```

Implicit returns even work with loops:

```
squareAll = (numbers) ->
  for n in numbers
    n * n
```

Here's the resulting JavaScript. See how it tracks and returns the resulting list?

```
squareAll = function(numbers) {
  var n, _i, _len, _results;
  _results = [];
  for (_i = 0, _len = numbers.length; _i < _len; _i++) {
    n = numbers[_i];
    _results.push(n * n);
  }
  return _results;
};
```

You certainly may continue using explicit returns if you wish, but idiomatic CoffeeScript avoids using return *unless it is necessary*. We will often use return to leave a function early if certain conditions are or aren't met:

```
middleElement = (list) ->
  return if list.length is 0
  list[Math.floor list.length / 2]
```

Or you may use it to break out of a loop:

```
firstSubstring = (stringToMatch, snippets) ->
  for substr in snippets
    return substr unless stringToMatch.indexOf(substr) is -1
  "No match :("
```

In this example, we use return to break out of the loop if we find a match. If the loop exits without a match, the function will reach the last statement, which implicitly returns "No match :(". Using return early in the function with a second implicit return at the end is a common pattern in idiomatic CoffeeScript.

If you want to make sure your function doesn't return a value, you can add an empty `return` to the end as follows:

```
sideEffectsOnly = (myArray) ->
  myArray.pop()
  return
```

Or you can place a `null` at the end, which will be implicitly returned:

```
sideEffectsOnly = (myArray) ->
  myArray.pop()
  null
```

Most of the time, though, you simply don't need to worry about it. Use the implicit return when you want it, ignore it when you don't. It may also encourage you to write more side-effect-free code, which is a good thing in general.

Adding dynamic behavior to our application

Now that we know how to define functions in CoffeeScript, we can add extra functionality to our application while keeping our code clean, modular, and easy to understand. The first change we will implement is to make the list clickable. When a customer clicks on a pet, they'll see a short description of the animal.

We'll add a container to `index.html` to hold the currently selected pet's description:

```
<!DOCTYPE html>
<html>
  <head>
    <title>The Pet Shop</title>
  </head>
  <body>
    <h1>Welcome to <span id="owner_name"></span>'s Pet Shop</h1>

    <p>We have some lovely pets available for the
    right owner to take home today. Please have a
    look at our selection.</p>

    <ul id="available_pets">
    </ul>
    <div id="pet_information">
    </div>
```

```
        <script src="setup.js"></script>
    </body>
</html>
```

Let's add some rules to our style sheet to cover all the elements we are going to add. Add these to `style.css`:

```
#available_pets {
    margin: 0;
    float: left;
    border-right: 1px solid #194900;
}
#available_pets li {
    list-style: none;
    margin: 0;
    padding: 0;
}
#available_pets li a {
    display: block;
    text-decoration: none;
    color: #194900;
    font-weight: bold;
    margin: 0.1em 0;
    padding: 0.5em 5em 0.5em 0.5em;
}
```

 I have omitted some of the rules here for brevity. Download the code for this chapter to get the full CSS. Visit http://www.packtpub. com/support and choose **CoffeeScript Application Development** from the dropdown.

We'll also need to add some extra information to our array of pets, so we have something to display:

```
shop = {
    owner: { name: "Ian" }
    animals: [
        name: "Kelsey"
        type: "dog"
        breed: "Labrador"
        description: "A sweet and loyal dog. Loves to play fetch.
Sometimes drinks out of the toilet."
        ,
        name: "Sgt. Snuffles"
        type: "dog"
```

```
    breed: "Pug"
    description: "Small in stature, but big in heart, Sgt.
Snuffles is never one to back down from a mission."
  ,
    name: "Chomps"
    type: "rabbit"
    breed: "Giant Angora"
    description: "Chomps is usually very good-natured, but he does
not take kindly to being mistaken for an ottoman. Come see him in
person and you'll understand why that may happen."
  #, ...
  ]
}
```

I've omitted some of the data here for brevity. Download the code for this chapter to get the full list of animals. Visit `http://www.packtpub.com/support` and choose **CoffeeScript Application Development** from the dropdown.

We're using a tricky bit of CoffeeScript syntax here. We can separate different objects within an array by using an **outdented comma** in between the objects. If you're not comfortable with this style, feel free to add curly braces around the individual objects. There's often more than one way to do a thing in CoffeeScript, and sometimes it's merely a matter of personal taste.

Now let's define the function that will turn a pet object into HTML to display:

```
formatPetDescription = (pet) ->
  "<h2>#{pet.name}</h2>" +
    "<h3 class='breed'>#{pet.breed}</h3>" +
    "<p class='description'>#{pet.description}</p>"
```

It's a fairly simple function. We construct a big string containing all of the pet's information, using string interpolation to keep it nice and neat. You can see that we're actually defining several strings and combining them with +. This is an easy way to split the string across several lines so that it doesn't wrap or scroll off the edge of the screen in some editors. The string is implicitly returned so that the caller can do something with the results.

We have a function that formats the object for display, but we still need code to put the pieces back together. Let's define another function. This one will be invoked when a pet is selected. The first thing we need it to do is find the appropriate pet object to pass to formatPetDescription.

Let's pass an array index to it and have it retrieve the object from `shop.animals`:

```
selectPet = (petIndex) ->
  pet = shop.animals[petIndex]
```

Next we'll pass the pet object to the function we defined to format it. And we'll insert the results into the container in our page as follows:

```
selectPet = (petIndex) ->
  pet = shop.animals[petIndex]
  petInfo = document.getElementById "pet_information"
  petInfo.innerHTML = formatPetDescription pet
```

This looks pretty good, but there's a problem. Remember how CoffeeScript makes sure that all variables are locally scoped? In this case, we need to be able to call this function from an `onclick` callback, so we will want it to be in the global scope. To do this, just attach the function to the `window` object:

```
window.selectPet = (petIndex) ->
  pet = shop.animals[petIndex]
  petInfo = document.getElementById "pet_information"
  petInfo.innerHTML = formatPetDescription pet
```

Let's add one final thing. We want to make it clear which item in the list is currently selected, so we'll give the selected link a class. This will let us apply some styling to tie it visually to the pet information box. When a new item is selected, we'll also need to loop through the elements in the list and remove our class from the previously selected item:

```
window.selectPet = (petIndex, element) ->
  pet = shop.animals[petIndex]
  petInfo = document.getElementById "pet_information"
  petInfo.innerHTML = formatPetDescription pet
  for link in document.querySelectorAll("#available_pets a")
    link.className = ""
  element.className = "selected"
```

> `document.querySelectorAll` is a modern-browser offering. It takes a string with CSS-style selectors and returns all DOM elements matching the selectors. Its counterpart, `document.querySelector`, does the same but only returns the first element found. This functionality is inspired by the popular jQuery library and is supremely useful. As you might expect, these native functions won't work on older browsers. If you need to support older browsers, you should use a compatibility library instead.

Okay! This function looks pretty good. The last thing we need to do is modify the HTML list that we generate to use links with `onclick` callbacks. Our function is expecting two arguments, an array index and the context of the event. To pass the correct array index, let's use the second argument to the `in` loop that we learned about in *Chapter 2, Writing Your First Lines of Coffeescript*.

```
petOutput = for pet, i in shop.animals
  "<li><a href='#' onclick='selectPet(#{i}, this)'>" +
  "#{pet.name}</a></li>"
```

Let's try it out! If you don't have your CoffeeScript compiler running in the background, invoke it with the following command:

coffee -c setup.coffee

Now load `index.html` in a browser. Try clicking on one of the pets, and you should see a result like the following screenshot:

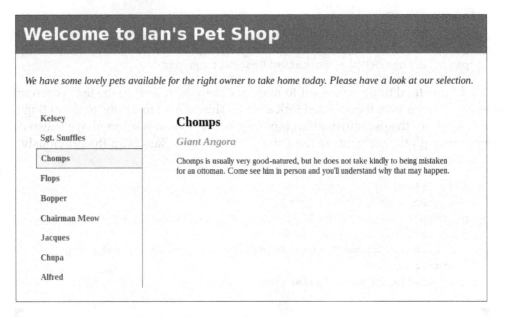

There's one more piece of functionality we would like to add in this chapter. To do it easily, we're going to want to use a new construct: the `switch` statement. It's time for another side trip into the unexplored lands of CoffeeScript features.

Switch statements

JavaScript offers `switch`/`case` statements as an alternative to wordy repetitions of `if`/`else-if`. You provide a value to `switch`, then attempt to match it against a series of patterns. The first matching block is executed. Unfortunately, JavaScript inherited its semantics from C, which comes with an unpleasant gotcha. If `break` is not specified at the end of a block, the code will continue through and execute the body of the next block as well. While this can be used intentionally by clever programmers to string together complex logic, more often than not it is used by accident when someone forgets a `break`. Let's take a look at an example:

```
switch (command) {
  case "build":
    compile();
    break;
  case "deploy":
    activate(REMOTE_SERVER);
    start_ftp();
    break;
  case "test":
    check_files();
    run_test_suite();
  case "NUKE":
    remove(ALL_THE_FILES);
    break;
  default:
    console.log("Unknown command");
}
```

What happens when someone passes `"test"` there? Do you think that's what the author intended to happen?

CoffeeScript offers a similar construct, but uses `switch`, `when`, and `else` as the keywords. `break` commands are automatically inserted.

```
switch iSpy
  when "sky"
    console.log "blue"
  when "grass"
    console.log "green"
  else
    console.log "gray"
```

This compiles to a well-formed JavaScript `switch`:

```
switch (iSpy) {
  case "sky":
    console.log("blue");
    break;
  case "grass":
    console.log("green");
    break;
  default:
    console.log("gray");
}
```

We may also shorten a block to a single line using `then`:

```
switch iSpy
  when "sky" then console.log "blue"
  when "grass" then console.log "green"
  else console.log "gray"
```

If you want to run the same block of code for several different patterns (the most common intentional use of JavaScript's fall-through mechanism), put the patterns in one `when` statement, separated by commas:

```
switch iSpy
  when "sky", "lake"
    console.log "blue"
  when "grass", "frog", "stoplight"
    console.log "green"
  else
    console.log "gray"
```

The generated JavaScript for this falls through in only the correct places:

```
switch (iSpy) {
  case "sky":
  case "lake":
    console.log("blue");
    break;
  case "grass":
  case "frog":
  case "stoplight":
    console.log("green");
    break;
  default:
    console.log("gray");
}
```

The other great feature of switch statements in CoffeeScript is that they can be assigned directly as expressions. Let's assign the output of a switch statement to a variable:

```
drivingAction = switch stoplightColor
  when "red" then "stop"
  when "yellow" then "slow down"
  else "go"
```

CoffeeScript achieves this by wrapping the `switch` in an anonymous function:

```
drivingAction = (function() {
  switch (stoplightColor) {
    case "red":
      return "stop";
    case "yellow":
      return "slow down";
    default:
      return "go";
  }
})();
```

Pretty clever, right?

Using a switch statement in our application

With the power of switch statements at our command, it's time to add another feature. Let's add an animal sound next to each pet in the list so that customers can scan the page for the types of pet they are interested in. We don't have the sounds in the animal objects that we've stored. However, we do have the type of animal each pet is, and we know what sounds each type of animal makes. We can generate the information we want dynamically, and `switch` is the perfect tool to do it.

First we'll define a function that takes an animal object and determines the sound that the animal makes:

```
animalSound = (animal) ->
  switch animal.type
    when "cat" then "meow"
    when "dog" then "bark"
    when "horse", "donkey"
      "neigh"
    else "sniff sniff"
```

 Okay, I admit it, I don't know what sounds rabbits make.

Next, we need to modify the loop that creates the pet links. Since the display rules for an animal's name are getting a little complex, and we may wish to reuse them elsewhere, let's pull those rules out into a separate function and invoke that function from our loop.

```
formatPetName = (pet) ->
  "#{pet.name} <span class='sound'>#{animalSound pet}!</span>"

petOutput = for pet, i in shop.animals
  "<li><a href='#' onclick='selectPet(#{i}, this)'>" +
  "#{formatPetName pet}</a></li>"
```

Great! Let's take a look in the browser and make sure everything looks good:

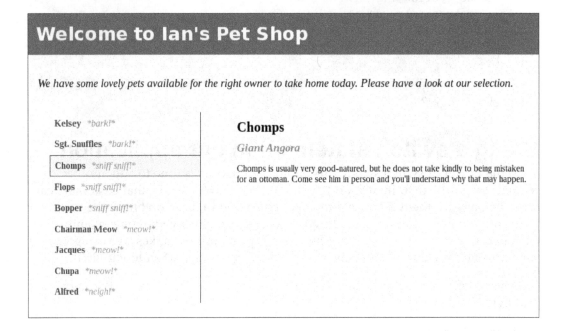

Perfect!

Summary

At the beginning of this chapter, we had a lot of knowledge but nothing to show for it. Now, we've got a snazzy single-page web application built with all the goodness of CoffeeScript! There's still a lot more that we can add to our application, but this is a pretty good start.

We learned:

- How to set up a CoffeeScript application to behave like a normal JavaScript application
- How to manipulate the DOM from CoffeeScript, and how to call back to CoffeeScript functions on events
- How to define functions in CoffeeScript, how to name them, and how implicit return values work
- How to use `switch` statements

Now that we've had a chance to flex our new CoffeeScript muscles, we're going to hit the gym again. We'll keep adding to our application as we go, but we've got a lot of new CoffeeScript syntax to learn! We'll explore some intermediate features of CoffeeScript, and use them in turn to improve our pet shop's web application.

4
Improving Our Application

We've built a nice little application for our pet store. Now it's time to get fancy! We're going to explore some of the more advanced features CoffeeScript has to offer. These features let you write code that is very concise — code that says what you *mean* to do and skips all the boilerplate. These features also help you write safer, less buggy code by taking the best practices and idioms that the community has settled on and baking them right into the syntax.

Of course, we wouldn't want to learn these new CoffeeScript skills without putting them to use! As we go, we'll be adding more features to our application that make it more colorful and put our CoffeeScript into practice.

In this chapter, we will:

- Learn how to deal with values that might be undefined
- Learn new ways to assign values to variables
- Learn some advanced syntax for function arguments
- Add and display more rich information for our pets, like age and photos
- Let visitors filter the pet list by kind of animal
- Show visitors a rotating banner with a featured pet

Checking if a value exists

Dealing with non-existent values is a common need in JavaScript. Most often, you'll find yourself checking a property that may or may not be defined on an object you're currently working with. Other times, you might be working with an optional function argument, or with the return value of a function that returns a null in certain conditions. In all of these cases, you will likely want to do *something* with your value, but may need to treat it differently if the value is null, so as not to raise errors.

A common way to deal with this in JavaScript is:

```
if (myVar) {
    // Do something only if myVar is defined
}
```

However, this is an oft-discussed source of bugs, since it will not run for other false-ish values, such as 0, "", or false. The preferred way to perform this check is safer, but clumsy:

```
if (typeof myVar != 'undefined') {
    // Do something only if myVar is defined
}
```

Using the existential operator

CoffeeScript has a helpful **existential operator** to deal with these situations correctly and cleanly. It is a simple ? symbol.

```
if yeti?
  "I want to believe"
```

Appending a ? to a variable tests it for existence. The code inside the if will only execute if yeti is defined. We can get fancier to see what this operator can do:

```
animalStatus = (animal) ->
  creatures = { ocelot: true, dodo: false }
  if creatures[animal]?
    if creatures[animal]
      "The #{animal} is alive and well."
    else
      "Oh no! The #{animal} is extinct!"
  else
    "The #{animal} isn't real."

animalStatus("ocelot")
animalStatus("dodo")
animalStatus("unicorn")
```

You can see that it will return true even for the other false-ish values, letting our code differentiate between an extinct animal (dodo, which is defined) and an imaginary one (unicorn, which is not defined).

This syntax is wonderfully concise, especially when testing the existence of multiple variables.

```
if hat? and mittens? and boots?
  goOutside()
```

We can check the compiled JavaScript to make sure it's doing the best thing:

```
if (typeof yeti !== "undefined" && yeti !== null) {
  "I want to believe";
}
```

Once again, CoffeeScript is careful to do the safe thing. First, it checks if the variable is defined. This is an important step before we try a comparison, since that would throw an error if the variable is not declared. If the variable is defined, it checks to see if it is null.

CoffeeScript will always be safe when necessary, but it knows to loosen up in other situations:

```
if (creatures[animal] != null) {
  //...
} else {
  //...
}
```

Since this one is an object access, there is no danger of throwing an error, so it simply checks if the value is equal to `null` or `undefined`.

Null values in chained calls

When dealing with a potentially null value, often the desirable course of action is to call a property or function on that value and return the result, or return null if the value is null. Unfortunately, calling any property on a null value results in an error, so you find yourself filling your code with `if` statements checking for existence. CoffeeScript offers a shorthand for this, using a variation on the existential operator.

```
trees =
  pine:
    type: "evergreen"
  crabapple:
    type: "deciduous"
    fruit:
      edible: false

if trees.pine.fruit?.edible
  console.log "Mmmm... pine fruit."
```

Normally, requesting `trees.pine.fruit.edible` would throw an error for attempting to read the `edible` property of an undefined value. However, using `?.` tells CoffeeScript to call the property *only* if the value exists. If the value does not exist, the expression evaluates to `undefined`.

We can chain several of these calls together if we are unsure of the existence of properties at several different levels:

```
if trees.truffula?.fruit?.edible
    console.log "Mmmm... truffula fruit."
```

We can combine a ? with square brackets for array and object access:

```
alpha =
    lowercase: ["a", "b", "c", "d"]
console.log alpha.lowercase?[2].toUpperCase()
console.log alpha.uppercase?[2].toLowerCase()

extractBugNumber = (line) ->
    line.match(/(issue|bug) #(\d+)/)?[2]
console.log extractBugNumber "This fixes bug #345."
console.log extractBugNumber "No bug number mentioned."
```

We can even combine ? with function calls:

```
oppositeMath =
    min: Math.max
console.log oppositeMath.min?(3, 2, 5)
console.log oppositeMath.max?(3, 2, 5)
```

Here the functions are only called if they exist. When they don't, the entire expression returns undefined.

Assigning new values conditionally when null

Another common desire when dealing with potentially null values is the ability to assign a different value *only* if the original value is null. Often we will have a default or fallback value that should be used if no value has been given. This is often handled in JavaScript with the || and ||= operators.

```
var briefcase = {};
briefcase.combination ||= "1234"
var payment = briefcase.contents || "credit"
```

However, this is still prone to the false-ish value problems that we discussed in the previous sections. And if we want to use a variable rather than an object property, we'll suffer from the errors that we discussed previously as well.

Since we have just finished learning about the ? operator in CoffeeScript, wouldn't it be nice if we could apply it to these situations as well? Good news, we can! Here's how we assign a new value only if the current value doesn't exist:

```
briefcase =
  color: "silver"
briefcase.combination ?= "1234"
briefcase.color ?= "black"
console.log briefcase
```

Please note that you cannot use an undeclared variable here. CoffeeScript will refuse to compile it because that variable is not a valid reference.

```
# Will not compile!
chupacabra ?= "coyote"
```

Here is an expression that will return the first value if it exists, and the second value otherwise:

```
sighting = mothMan ? "sandhill crane"
console.log sighting
```

This is similar to ?=, but is useful when you wish to send the value somewhere else rather than overwriting the potentially null variable.

If the ||= behavior is truly what you want, the ||= operator is still available to you. Remember when we learned about CoffeeScript language-based comparison operators? Those extend here too, so you can use or= instead for the same behavior.

```
ufosExist ||= wasAbducted
ufosExist or= saucerSpotted
```

Dealing with nulls in our application

We're going to add some new properties to our pet information. The first one we'll add is the pet's age. Since some pets at our shop are adopted from various sources, we don't always know the age of the animal, but we'd like to show it when we do.

First, we'll add an age property to some of the animals in our list:

```
animals: [
  name: "Kelsey"
  type: "dog"
  age: 2
  breed: "Labrador"
```

```
      description: "A sweet and loyal dog. Loves to play fetch. Sometimes
    drinks out of the toilet."
  ,
  ...
    name: "Flops"
    type: "rabbit"
    age: 4
  ...
    name: "Jacques"
    type: "cat"
    age: 11
  ...
    name: "Chupa"
    type: "cat"
    age: 3
  ...
  ]
```

Now, let's add some text in the pet description next to the breed. It should give the pet's age if the value exists, and otherwise show question marks. This is a perfect use of our existential operator!

```
formatPetDescription = (pet) ->
  "<h2>#{pet.name}</h2>" +
    "<h3 class='breed'>#{pet.breed} " +
    "(#{pet.age ? "??"} years old)</h3>" +
    "<p class='description'>#{pet.description}</p>"
```

We'll use `pet.age` if it exists, and fill in with **??** if it does not. Once we reload our application, if we choose a pet with an age listed, it should look like this:

Kelsey

Labrador (2 years old)

A sweet and loyal dog. Loves to play fetch. Sometimes drinks out of the toilet.

If we choose a pet without an age listed, we should see the fallback:

> ## Chomps
>
> *Giant Angora (?? years old)*
>
> Chomps is usually very good-natured, but he does not take kindly to being mistaken for an ottoman. Come see him in person and you'll understand why that may happen.

Now let's add one more property to our pets list. We have photos of some of the pets, and would like to display those in the description as well. Once again, we only have photos for some of the pets, so we'll need to display a photo if it's present, and carry on gracefully if it is not. We'll start out by adding the photo file names to our `animals` array:

```
name: "Flops"
type: "rabbit"
age: 4
breed: "French Lop"
image: "flops.jpg"
...
name: "Chupa"
type: "cat"
age: 3
breed: "Scottish Fold"
image: "chupa.jpg"
...
```

We'll also need to store our photos with our application. Let's make an `images` directory and put them in there. Feel free to acquire your own photos if you wish, just make sure they are given the correct names. If you're using the sample code accompanying this book, you'll find the images I used included.

Now that we have the photos and the property set on the animal object, all we need to do is output an image tag in the pet description. We'll call a new function from `formatPetDescription`:

```
formatPetDescription = (pet) ->
  "<h2>#{pet.name}</h2>" +
    "<h3 class='breed'>#{pet.breed} " +
    "(#{pet.age ? "??"} years old)</h3>" +
    imageTag(pet.image) +
    "<p class='description'>#{pet.description}</p>"
```

Let's define our `imageTag` function. It will take one argument, but remember, that argument may be `undefined` if the current pet doesn't have a photo. Once again, we can use the existential operator. This time we will use it to only print out an `img` tag if a filename exists.

```
imageTag = (filename) ->
  if filename?
    "<img src='images/#{filename}' />"
  else
    ""
```

Now, when we reload our app and choose a pet with a photo, we should see it in the description, like this:

Chupa

Scottish Fold (3 years old)

Chupa always appears perplexed with the world, but don't be fooled. That's just the way his face is shaped.

Dealing with undefined values is an extremely useful ability, so we'll definitely be seeing these operators some more throughout the book. For now, though, it's time to move on to another useful CoffeeScript feature: a structured form of variable assignment.

Assigning multiple values at once

Let's look at a handy shorthand for assigning values to variables. CoffeeScript offers a feature called **destructuring assignment**. This is a fancy term that means you can assign multiple variables from an array or object using a single expression.

```
[first, second] = ["horse", "cart"]
console.log "Don't put the #{second} before the #{first}."
```

We were able to assign the variables first and second in one expression simply by adding square brackets around them. Looking at the compiled JavaScript shows us how CoffeeScript achieves this:

```
_ref = ["horse", "cart"], first = _ref[0], second = _ref[1];
```

It's using a temporary variable for reference, and then assigning the variables one at a time using array indexes. This looks very much like the code we might write by hand to do this if we weren't lucky enough to be using CoffeeScript.

You might choose to use this syntax simply for convenience when initializing some values:

```
[login, password] = ["admin", "r00tsh3ll"]
```

Or you might use it because it is the most meaningful way to express what you're doing:

```
[x, y] = [22, 15]
hypotenuse = Math.sqrt x*x + y*y
```

Or we might use it because we are calling a function that returns multiple values. For example, this regular expression will match a language ending in *Script*. We are interested in the first subgroup, so we'll separate the return value:

```
[languageName, prefix] = "CoffeeScript".match /(.*)Script/
console.log "I love the smell of #{prefix} in the morning."
```

We can even use destructuring assignment to perform in-place variable swaps:

```
[first, second] = ["cow", "milk"]
# Wait, or is it the other way around?
[first, second] = [second, first]
console.log "Don't put the #{second} before the #{first}."
```

Destructuring assignment can be used with more complicated structures too:

```
[drink, [alcohol, mixer]] = ["Screwdriver", ["vodka", "orange juice"]]
console.log "A #{drink} consists of #{alcohol} and #{mixer}."
```

It can even be used on objects. We can either give our variable the name as the key we wish to retrieve:

```
blackbird = verb: "singing", time: "midnight"
{time} = blackbird
console.log "At #{time}"
```

Or we can give the key and then our variable name:

```
{verb: birdBehavior} = blackbird
console.log "It was #{birdBehavior}."
```

We can nest objects within each other and pull out only the keys we are interested in:

```
retroGames =
  pacman:
    villains: "ghosts"
    objective: "eat dots"
  spaceInvaders:
    villains: "aliens"
    objective: "shoot aliens"

{
  pacman: {villains, objective},
  spaceInvaders: { villains: otherBadGuys}
} = retroGames

console.log "In Pacman the goal was to #{objective}."
console.log "The enemies were #{villains}. At least they weren't
#{otherBadGuys}."
```

We can nest arrays inside of objects, and vice versa:

```
boat = { directions: ["port", "starboard"] }
{directions: [left, right]} = boat
console.log "Turn to #{right}!"
```

```
directionCommands = [
  {type: "boat", directions: ["port", "starboard"]},
  {type: "dogsled", directions: ["haw", "gee"]}
]
[boatInfo, {directions: [left, right]}] = directionCommands
console.log "#{left}! Mush!"
```

A word of caution: try not to get carried away with nested assignments. This tool is very handy from time to time, but it can quickly become confusing if overused. If you find yourself frequently manipulating large, deeply-nested objects, take a moment to reconsider the architecture of your application. You may have found a good opportunity to simplify your code by tweaking how you structure your data, or by splitting different concerns out into smaller, more focused functions.

Using destructuring assignment in our application

We decided it's a little silly to require an animal sound for every type of animal. After all, rabbits don't make any recognizable sounds. Instead, let's alter our function to return both a sound *and* an action, either of which may be null. We'll leave it up to the formatting function to decide whether to use one or both of the values we return. First, we'll modify `animalSound` to return a two-element array (often called a **duple**) of a sound and an action. We'll also rename the function to reflect this change.

```
animalBehaviors = (animal) ->
  switch animal.type
    when "cat" then ["meow", null]
    when "dog" then ["bark", "wag"]
    when "rabbit" then [null, "hop hop"]
    when "horse", "donkey"
      ["neigh", null]
    else
      [null, null]
```

In `formatPetName`, we will receive this duple and use destructuring assignment to easily access the values. Let's show the `sound` if it exists, and if not fall back to the `action`.

```
formatPetName = (pet) ->
  [sound, action] = animalBehaviors pet
  [behavior, cssClass] = if sound?
    ["#{sound}!", "sound"]
  else
    [action, "action"]

  "#{pet.name} " +
    "<span class='#{cssClass}'>#{behavior.toLowerCase()}</span>"
```

Once again, we find a use for the existential operator that we learned about in the previous section. Besides the sound or action itself, we also want to vary the CSS class assigned to the containing span. This gives us another chance to use destructuring assignment. Since we have set the CSS class nicely, we can now modify our CSS style sheet so it includes the `.action` selector, and we can upgrade the CSS so it shows quote marks around sounds, and stars around actions.

```
#available_pets li a .sound,
#available_pets li a .action {
  margin-left: 0.4em;
  font-weight: normal;
  font-style: italic;
  color: gray;
}

#available_pets li a .action:before,
#available_pets li a .action:after {
  content: "*";
}

#available_pets li a .sound:before,
#available_pets li a .sound:after {
  content: '"';
}
```

Your pet list should now look like this:

> **Kelsey** *"bark!"*
>
> **Sgt. Snuffles** *"bark!"*
>
> **Chomps** **hop hop**
>
> **Flops** **hop hop**
>
> **Bopper** **hop hop**
>
> **Chairman Meow** *"meow!"*
>
> **Jacques** *"meow!"*
>
> **Chupa** *"meow!"*
>
> **Alfred** *"neigh!"*

Advanced function arguments

It's fairly common when defining functions to find that your code will be easiest to use if you offer some flexibility in your **function signatures**—particularly in the arguments that are passed to a function. Some arguments to a function may be optional, and it's nice to let your caller pass only the information that is relevant to that specific invocation of the function.

Most modern programming languages offer some way to achieve this. JavaScript is no exception, though its mechanisms for doing so are slightly arcane. If you have ever wanted to allow an optional argument in JavaScript, you may have written some code like this to do it:

```
/*
 * formatTemperature(degrees, scale='K')
 */
function formatTemperature(degrees, scale) {
  if (typeof scale === "undefined") {
    scale = "K";
  }
  var formatted = degrees.toFixed(1);
  formatted += (scale.toUpperCase() === 'K') ? " " : "°";
  return formatted + scale.toUpperCase();
}
console.log(formatTemperature(22, "C"));
console.log(formatTemperature(42.55));
```

The scale argument is optional, despite being declared as a regular argument in the function definition. Since JavaScript is lax about enforcing the number of arguments passed to a function invocation, we simply check to see if scale is undefined, and set a default if so.

And if you have ever wanted to define a function that takes *any* number of arguments, you may have written some code like this:

```
function formattedAverageTemperature(scale /*, temperatures...*/) {
  var sum = 0;
  for (i=1; i<arguments.length; i++) {
    sum += arguments[i];
  }
  return formatTemperature(sum / (arguments.length - 1), scale)
}
console.log(formattedAverageTemperature("F", 98, 10, 32));
```

Here we use the arguments object, which always contains all arguments passed to the current function. You can see that the required first argument complicated matters a bit. Our for loop and the length value in the denominator both had to account for the offset starting position. Dealing with these situations by hand is possible, but it's never very enjoyable. Fiddling with the arguments object is the work you *have* to do before you can get to the work you *want* to do.

These examples also demonstrated two ways that you might document extra arguments in JavaScript using comments. It's good practice to do so — this improves the experience for anyone else who wishes to read your code. Without documentation, the only way to find out about these special arguments is to read and understand the entire code block, which is asking a lot of someone who simply wants to call your function. The comments put this information back in (or at least close to) the function signature, where it belongs.

Documenting these arguments in comments, while better than nothing, still suffers from a serious flaw: they are comments. It's incredibly easy for a comment to get out of sync with the actual code. All it takes is one inattentive or rushed developer changing the code without changing the accompanying comment, and your code now has undocumented, or worse, *inaccurately documented* behavior.

A comment is a lie waiting to happen. – Alex Chaffee

As usual, CoffeeScript has the answer. We'll explore some syntax CoffeeScript offers to deal with these exact problems. We'll be able to put argument information back into the function signature, and at the same time have our arguments assigned properly without any intervention.

Default argument values

First, let's look at default arguments. These are a great way to define a function that is very simple to call in the most common case, but can be customized with additional options for the uncommon cases. Let's take our first example from the previous section, a function that returns a formatted temperature, and rewrite it in CoffeeScript.

```coffeescript
formatTemperature = (degrees, scale='K') ->
  formatted = degrees.toFixed 1
  formatted += if scale.toUpperCase() is 'K' then " " else "°"
  formatted + scale.toUpperCase()

console.log formatTemperature(22.35, "C")
console.log formatTemperature(42)
```

This looks similar, but in the arguments list, we've declared `scale` with a default value. If a value is not passed when the function is called, it will be assigned the default automatically. We were able to remove the entire `if` statement we used in JavaScript to assign this default. If we check the compiled JavaScript for this code, we'll see that the generated function looks a lot like what we started with:

```javascript
var formatTemperature;
formatTemperature = function(degrees, scale) {
  var formatted;
  if (scale == null) {
    scale = 'K';
  }
  formatted = degrees.toFixed(1);
  formatted += scale.toUpperCase() === 'K' ? " " : "°";
  return formatted + scale.toUpperCase();
};
```

In this instance, CoffeeScript has created code that is subtly better than my original version. I used `if (typeof scale === "undefined")` to test for the existence of my argument. CoffeeScript uses `if (scale == null)` instead. Why does this work? We are in the habit of checking the type of variables, because a comparison with an undeclared variable will result in an error. In this situation, though, the variable is always declared, since it's in the function signature. The only two values that (with type coercion) are considered equal to `null` are `null` and `undefined`, so there will be no accidents if the value is `0`, `""`, or `false`.

Comparing to `null` gains us one extra advantage. This allows the caller to pass a `null` explicitly to the function to make sure that the default value is used. In our next example, if we wanted to call `formatTemperature` with a special value for `decimalPlaces`, but wanted to make sure it used the default value for `scale`, we could call it like this:

```
console.log formatTemperature(88.11265, null, 4)
```

By thinking carefully about the context, CoffeeScript was able to achieve the same behavior as the `typeof` construction, with one helpful exception that makes it easier to call functions with optional arguments.

We can use multiple optional arguments in a single function signature, too. They will be filled in from left to right as more arguments are passed. Let's add another optional argument to change the number of decimal places displayed in our temperature:

```
formatTemperature = (degrees, scale='K', decimalPlaces=1) ->
  formatted = degrees.toFixed decimalPlaces
  formatted += if scale.toUpperCase() is 'K' then " " else "°"
  formatted + scale.toUpperCase()

console.log formatTemperature(42)
console.log formatTemperature(22.35, "C")
console.log formatTemperature(12.34, "F", 2)
```

Using default arguments in our application

It's time to add another feature to our application. This time, we want to give visitors a little more control over their viewing experience. Many people who come to our site are only interested in one particular type of animal. Rabbits, maybe. Those people would appreciate an option to filter the list of available pets so it shows only the type of animal they are interested in seeing.

We'll add a new element to `index.html` to hold the filtering options:

```html
<div id="filtering">
  <span class="instructions">Filter by animal type:</span>
  <ul id="filtering_opts">
  </ul>
</div>
<ul id="available_pets">
...
```

And we'll add some CSS to make it look nice:

```css
#filtering {
  margin: 1em;
  background: #F2EDDE;
  padding: 0.5em;
  border-radius: 0.5em;
  overflow: auto;
}
#filtering ul, #filtering li, #filtering .instructions {
  float: left;
}
#filtering ul {
  list-style: none;
  margin: 0;
  padding: 0;
}
#filtering li {
  margin: 0 0.5em;
}
#filtering a {
  color: #333;
}
```

Next we'll write some CoffeeScript to build the list of filtering links. We could pull the available types out of our `animals` array, but coding the array by hand will save us some iteration and allow us to control the order. For each animal type, we'll create a link with a callback to a new function.

```coffeescript
filteringOutput = for type in ["All", "Dog", "Cat", "Rabbit", "Horse"]
  "<li><a href='#' onclick='displayPetList(\"#{type}\")'>#{type}</a>
</li>"

filteringOpts = document.getElementById("filtering_opts")
filteringOpts.innerHTML = filteringOutput.join ""
```

Finally, we'll define the callback function to display a filtered list of pets. We already wrote the code to generate a pet list, we just need to modify it a little. First, since we're going to be dynamically re-rendering the pet list, we'll want to refactor that code into a function. Second, we'll want to add an argument for the type of animal to display.

```
window.displayPetList = (filter="All") ->
  petOutput = for pet, i in shop.animals when filter is "All" or
filter.toLowerCase() is pet.type
    "<li><a href='#' onclick='selectPet(#{i}, this)'>#{formatPetName
pet}</a></li>"

  availablePets = document.getElementById("available_pets")
  availablePets.innerHTML = petOutput.join ""

window.displayPetList()
```

Our function is attached to `window` so that it is available to the `onclick` callback. Remember, all variables are locally scoped in CoffeeScript unless we set them otherwise.

We defined `filter` as an optional argument. This way, we may call it later with no arguments to get the default behavior (in this case, displaying all animal types). We compare the value of filter in the guard on our for loop, only accepting types that match it (unless the filter is "All"). After defining the function, we call it once so the list will be displayed on page load.

That's it! Our application should now show filtering options along the top, and when clicked, it should filter the list to the chosen animal type.

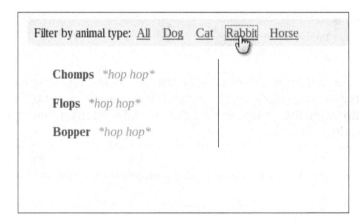

Accepting a variable number of arguments with splats

Now let's talk about a slightly different situation—one where we need to accept an open-ended number of arguments. Usually we will be acting on these arguments as a list, but it's often nice to let the caller pass them directly without creating an array. We wrote a function that behaves this way at the beginning of the chapter, so let's rewrite it in CoffeeScript using a new feature, **splats**.

```
formattedAverageTemperature = (scale, temperatures...) ->
  sum = 0
  sum += t for t in temperatures
  formatTemperature(sum / (temperatures.length), scale)

console.log formattedAverageTemperature("F", 98, 10, 32)
```

Appending . . . to an argument name in the function definition tells CoffeeScript to accept any number of arguments. That variable will be assigned an array containing all the relevant values that were passed. We iterate through `temperatures` to add up all the values, and later check its `length` property to calculate the average. This time we don't need to manipulate `temperatures` to remove the first value for `scale`— CoffeeScript took care of all that for us!

The compiled JavaScript version of this function works carefully with `arguments` to achieve this:

```
var formattedAverageTemperature, __slice = [].slice;
formattedAverageTemperature = function() {
  var scale, sum, t, temperatures, _i, _len;
  scale = arguments[0];
  temperatures = 2<=arguments.length ? __slice.call(arguments, 1) :
[];
  sum = 0;
  for (_i = 0, _len = temperatures.length; _i < _len; _i++) {
    t = temperatures[_i];
    sum += t;
  }
  return formatTemperature(sum / temperatures.length, scale);
};
```

You can see another small CoffeeScript helper at the top, where `slice` is pulled out of the `Array` instance methods and saved as `__slice`. CoffeeScript uses this to extract the correct values for `temperatures`. Notice that it will even set an empty array if the splat receives no arguments. This lets us keep things concise, and helps prevent nasty errors from code trying to iterate on an undefined value.

A splat will work even if it is not the last argument. This is extremely helpful when working with asynchronous libraries, in which functions take a callback that by convention is always the last argument.

```
fetchSearchResults = (url, searchTerms..., callback) ->
  console.log "Searching #{url} for #{searchTerms.join " "} now."
  asyncRequest url, buildQuery(searchTerms), callback
```

We can even use splats as a part of a destructuring assignment, the useful shorthand we learned earlier in the chapter. We can capture part of a data structure as an array, just like we would in function arguments.

```
[race, [splits..., time]] = ["10k", ["13:08", "13:09", "26:17"]]
console.log "The world record for #{race} is #{time}."
console.log "The splits were #{splits.join " and "}."
```

Cool, huh?

Invoking functions with splats

Not only can we use splats when defining functions, we can use them when calling functions as well. Let's call our formattedAverageTemperature function, but pass it an array of values we're storing in a variable.

```
temps = [-10, 44, 80]
console.log formattedAverageTemperature("F", temps...)
```

We can use this not only for our own functions, but for library functions or standard JavaScript functions—anything that takes multiple arguments. We can use it to call Math.min on an unspecified number of values:

```
formattedColdestTemperature = (scale, temperatures...) ->
  minTemp = Math.min temperatures...
  formatTemperature(minTemp, scale)
console.log formattedColdestTemperature "C", 20, -5, 33
```

It can be a little confusing at first to remember what a splat does in each situation. Think of it this way: the splat is always going to let *you* deal with an array. If the splat is *incoming* to the arguments of a function you're in, the data comes in as separate values and reaches you as an array. If the splat is *outgoing* to a function you're calling, it will leave you as an array and reach the function as separate values.

Using splats in our application

Let's add another feature to our application. We've decided that the introduction paragraph isn't necessary, and is taking up space that could be used to promote the pets we most want to find a home. Let's replace that paragraph with a new section where we spotlight a featured pet. We'll specify several pets, and our application can randomly cycle through them every time the page is loaded.

As usual, we'll add a container for this new feature. This will go in place of the old paragraph of text:

```
<h1>Welcome to <span id="owner_name"></span>'s Pet Shop</h1>
<div id="featured">
</div>
<div id="filtering">
```

And we'll add some CSS so that our new feature fits in with the rest of the site:

```
#featured {
  margin: 1em;
  background: #F2EDDE;
  padding: 0.5em;
  border-radius: 0.5em;
  width: 15em;
  border: 3px solid #C93F00;
}

#featured .title {
  font-weight: bold;
  display: block;
  margin: 0.2em 0 0.5em 0;
}

#featured a {
  font-weight: bold;
  text-decoration: none;
  margin: 0.3em 0;
  display: block;
  color: #890900;
}
```

We'll want this new feature to hold a link that displays the pet's description when clicked. We already have some code in `displayPetList` to output a link with a callback, so let's reuse that. We'll need to factor that code out of `displayPetList` into its own function.

```
formatPetLink = (pet, i) ->
  "<a href='#' onclick='selectPet(#{i}, this)'>" +
  "#{formatPetName pet}</a>"
```

 Make sure to declare this function before `displayPetList` in the file.

This function takes two arguments, a pet object and an index, and constructs an anchor tag. Now we'll refactor the first part of `displayPetList` to use this function:

```
window.displayPetList = (filter="All") ->
  petOutput = for pet, i in shop.animals when filter is "All" or
filter.toLowerCase() is pet.type
    "<li>#{formatPetLink pet, i}</li>"
...
```

Now `formatPetLink` is ready for us to use, so let's build a function to display the featured pets. We'll start with what we want our function call to look like:

```
displayFeatured "Chupa", "Kelsey", "Flops"
```

It should take any number of pet names, randomly choose one, and display it in the featured slot. How should we make this possible? Why, by using a splat, of course!

```
displayFeatured = (featuredPets...) ->
```

Having declared this argument, we now have an array of pet names to work with. Let's step through the rest of the function line-by-line. First we need to choose a random name from the list.

```
chosenPetIndex = Math.floor Math.random() * featuredPets.length
chosenPetName = featuredPets[chosenPetIndex]
```

This is a common way to choose a random number in CoffeeScript and JavaScript. `Math.random()` returns a float between 0 and 1. We multiply that by the number of items in our array, and round down to the nearest integer. This gives us a number between 0 and the last index in our array (the math works out nicely with 0-indexing). Then we simply pull the selected name out of our array.

Next we need to use this name to find the full pet object from our list of pets. This will allow us to call a callback to show the pet's description.

```
for pet, i in shop.animals when pet.name is chosenPetName
  [chosenPet, fullListIndex] = [pet, i]
```

We're looping through `shop.animals` with a guard to pick only the object with a `name` property equal to our chosen name. This should match exactly one item in the list, and when it does we save the object and index. Destructuring assignment lets us do this neatly on a single line.

Now we will insert the HTML for this feature into the container we set aside for it.

```
featured = document.getElementById("featured")
featured.innerHTML = "<span class='title'>Featured Pet</span>" +
  formatPetLink chosenPet, fullListIndex
```

There! We're reusing the `formatPetLink` function that we defined earlier. This way we can display the pet description when a visitor clicks on the featured pet's name, and we don't have to add extra code to do it.

Putting this all together, our finished code looks like this:

```
displayFeatured = (featuredPets...) ->
  chosenPetIndex = Math.floor Math.random() * featuredPets.length
  chosenPetName = featuredPets[chosenPetIndex]
  for pet, i in shop.animals when pet.name is chosenPetName
    [chosenPet, fullListIndex] = [pet, i]
  featured = document.getElementById("featured")
  featured.innerHTML = "<span class='title'>Featured Pet</span>" +
    formatPetLink chosenPet, fullListIndex

displayFeatured "Chupa", "Kelsey", "Flops"
```

Let's try it out. Reloading our application shows us a featured pet box like this:

Nice! Let's make one more small change. When we're displaying the pet link in the featured box, we don't want to display the sound or action like we do in the full list below. In fact, our code can skip the work of looking up the animal's behavior when it's formatting for the featured box. We can keep using the same function to build the link; we just need to give it an extra argument to toggle the behavior display on or off.

```
formatPetLink = (pet, i, showBehavior=true) ->
  "<a href='#' onclick='selectPet(#{i}, this)'>" +
    "#{formatPetName pet, showBehavior}</a>"
```

We've given `formatPetLink` an optional argument that defaults to `true`. This way our old code will continue to work without changes, and we only need to modify the call from the featured display code. This function passes the toggle through to `formatPetName`, which is where the logic changes:

```
formatPetName = (pet, showBehavior) ->
  result = pet.name
  if showBehavior
    [sound, action] = animalBehaviors pet
    [behavior, cssClass] = if sound?
      ["#{sound}!", "sound"]
    else
      [action, "action"]

    result += " <span class='#{cssClass}'>#{behavior.toLowerCase()}</span>"
  result
```

This function will always render the pet name, but will only append the behavior display if `showBehavior` is true. Finally, we will update the call in `displayFeatured` to pass false for this argument:

```
featured.innerHTML = "<span class='title'>Featured Pet:</span>"+
  formatPetLink chosenPet, fullListIndex, false
```

Let's try it out! Reload the application, and the featured box only shows the pet name:

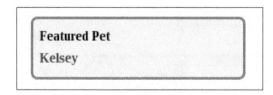

Featured Pet
Kelsey

If we try reloading a number of times, all the pets we passed to the function will show up. Clicking on the pet in this box will show its description down below.

Summary

This chapter was all about digging a little deeper into what CoffeeScript has to offer. We:

- Learned how to use the existential operator to deal with null and undefined values
- Learned how destructuring assignment lets us assign multiple values at once
- Learned how to give function arguments default values
- Learned how to receive and send multiple function arguments as arrays using splats

As we learned each of these concepts, we put them to use in our application. Along the way, we added some great new features to our pet store.

You may have noticed that our code base is growing larger, and sometime soon we'll be wanting a bit more organization. The next two chapters are all about that. We'll be looking at classes in CoffeeScript and how they can help us keep our code modular and understandable.

5

Classes in CoffeeScript

We're going to change gears for a bit in this chapter. We've been learning details of the CoffeeScript language and putting them to work in our pet store application. In this chapter, we'll take a step back and learn about a big concept: classes. We won't be working on the pet shop application in this chapter—instead we'll use small self-contained examples to explore how classes work. We haven't forgotten about the pet shop, though, and classes will certainly come in handy when we return to it!

In this chapter, we'll learn:

- What a class looks like in CoffeeScript
- How to attach functions and properties to it, and how to use them
- How to use inheritance to build powerful class hierarchies
- How all of this translates to clean, sensible JavaScript

Defining a class in CoffeeScript

A class, in essence, is not much more than a name and a collection of properties that define its behavior. A class is defined once, but can be **instantiated** many times.

Here's the simplest class definition in CoffeeScript:

```
class Airplane
```

That's it! We now have an `Airplane` class, and we can create instances of it.

```
plane = new Airplane()
plane.color = "white"
```

The `new` keyword instantiates the object just like in JavaScript. The parentheses are optional, but I prefer to leave them in, to keep it consistent with other function invocations with no arguments. We can set arbitrary properties on our plane, just as we can do with any object in JavaScript.

Attaching methods to a class

So far we haven't done much we couldn't accomplish just as well with a generic object. Let's attach a method to our class' prototype.

 A **method** is just a function that's attached to an object.

```
class Airplane
  takeOff: ->
    console.log "Vrrrroooom!"
```

Now we're making progress! CoffeeScript mimics the object syntax to attach methods to a class, since what we're doing is similar in concept. We could write something very similar using a generic object:

```
hangGlider =
  takeOff: ->
    console.log "Jump!"
```

However, *that* method is only attached to this one object. Our `Airplane` class can be instantiated multiple times, and every created object will have a `takeOff` method.

```
plane = new Airplane()
plane2 = new Airplane()
plane.takeOff()
plane2.takeOff()
```

The methods here are standard CoffeeScript definitions. Thus, if we wish to accept arguments, we use the same syntax as before:

```
class Airplane
  takeOff: (eta) ->
    console.log "#{s}..." for s in [eta..0]
    console.log "Vrrrroooom!"

plane = new Airplane()
plane.takeOff(7)
```

You can see that we have declared `takeOff` exactly like we would have declared a function that wasn't attached to an object. This method takes one argument, the number of seconds to go, and it prints a countdown before taking off.

How CoffeeScript builds classes in JavaScript

CoffeeScript's class system certainly looks nice, but its implementation is an important consideration. Classes and inheritance can trigger some weird behavior, especially in a language like JavaScript that uses **prototypal inheritance** instead of **classical inheritance**. We'll pause for a moment to find out just how CoffeeScript is achieving all this class stuff, and what it means for our projects.

We've seen in previous chapters that one of CoffeeScript's strengths is that it stays true to the core mechanics of JavaScript while cleaning up the syntax. This is precisely the case with the class system as well. CoffeeScript builds its classes on the best practices developed by the JavaScript community over the years, with a system that is simple, predictable and robust. If you're expecting CoffeeScript classes to spirit you away to a land of flawless classical inheritance, you may be slightly disappointed. But if you want a lightweight system with known behavior, CoffeeScript's classes fit the bill.

Let's look at the generated JavaScript for the Airplane model we defined earlier in the chapter:

```
var Airplane;
Airplane = (function() {

  function Airplane() {}

  Airplane.prototype.takeOff = function() {
    return console.log("Vrrrroooom!");
  };

  return Airplane;

})();
plane = new Airplane();
```

Looks a bit different, doesn't it? Let's look at how it's built. First we have `function Airplane() {}`. This is the heart of our class, a named `Function` object. After declaring that, the `takeOff` method is attached to `Airplane`'s prototype. All this is wrapped inside a function that returns the named `Airplane` object. This return value is assigned to the `Airplane` variable in the outer scope. This variable now contains the `Function` with an augmented prototype, which will be passed to each object we instantiate with `new Airplane()`.

Prototypes are the key to JavaScript's class-like abilities. Every object has a prototype (which is essentially another object). When a property or method is accessed, an object first checks its own properties. If it doesn't find the requested reference, it then checks its prototype for the reference. When we call `plane.takeOff()`, the plane object doesn't have a `takeOff` method, so it passes the request to its prototype, which does. This is how the methods we attach to a class are available to every instance of that class.

Maintaining state with object properties

One of the important things objects do is maintain **state**. This lets us give values to an instance of a class that it will remember and use to determine its output and behavior. State is stored in properties attached to the object. We attached a color property to our plane object earlier, but we haven't yet accessed it from within the object's own methods. We can accomplish this using the @ operator. Let's provide a description of our plane that includes its color:

```
class Airplane
  describe: ->
    "A #{@color} plane"

plane = new Airplane()
plane.color = "white"
console.log plane.describe()
```

We set the color of the plane after creating the object. When we call `describe`, the property we set is available to the method by accessing `@color`. These properties are independent to each object instance:

```
plane2 = new Airplane()
plane2.color = "blue"
console.log plane2.describe()
```

The second plane's state is maintained separate from the first plane's state... of course! This is what makes objects so useful.

Calling other methods on this object

Within an object's method, we may also want to call another method on that object. Once again, we can use the @ operator for this.

```
class Airplane
  takeOff: (eta) ->
    @taxi()
```

```
      console.log "#{s}..." for s in [eta..0]
      console.log "Vrrrroooom!"
    taxi: ->
    if Math.random() > 0.5
      console.log "Taxiing..."
```

Our `takeOff` method now calls another method, `taxi`. Half the time, we'll need to taxi into position before we're ready to take off, and calling `@taxi()` takes care of that.

How does this all work? Well, `@something` is actually just an alias for `this.something`. Remember how we saw that CoffeeScript classes keep it simple on the JavaScript side? That still applies. Because we're using a standard JavaScript class structure, everything attached to our object is available through `this`. Looking at the generated JavaScript for our `Airplane` class, we can see the object property:

```
Airplane.prototype.describe = function() {
  return "A " + this.color + " plane";
};
```

And the object method invocation:

```
Airplane.prototype.takeOff = function(eta) {
  this.taxi();
  //...
};
```

We could, if we wanted, even replace the occurrences of `@` in our code with `this`. The `@` is simply a nice shorthand. This simplicity also means that CoffeeScript classes will behave predictably, and we won't have any friction if we need to use CoffeeScript code and JavaScript code together.

It's even possible, though rare, to use `@` by itself to pass `this` to another function. We might do this when calling an outside function that expects our entire object:

```
class Airplane
  parkAt: (airport) ->
    airport.store @

class Airport
  store: (plane) ->
    @hangar ?= []
    @hangar.push plane

chicago_ohare = new Airport()
plane.parkAt chicago_ohare
```

It might look a little funny to pass @ around by itself, but given a little time you'll get used to it. If you prefer, feel free to pass `this` in these situations for clarity, and use @ only to prefix methods and properties.

Attaching a method outside of the class definition

Most of the time, you will define your methods in the main body of the class definition. This is the easiest and most logical place. However, there are a few occasions when you may wish to attach a method to an object prototype from somewhere else in the code. This may be for stylistic or metaprogramming reasons, or most likely, to attach methods to an object that you did not define. CoffeeScript provides the `::` operator for easy access to an object's prototype. Let's attach our own method to `Date` to calculate the year according to Isaac Asimov's **Atomic Era (AE)**, which begins on December 1, 1944 CE.

```
Date::getYearAE = ->
  monthOffset = if @getMonth() < 11 then 1 else 0
  @getFullYear() - 1944 - monthOffset

today = new Date()
console.log "It is the year #{today.getYearAE()} AE"
```

We've successfully attached a new method to `Date`'s prototype, and it is now available for all `Date` objects.

 Be very careful when modifying native JavaScript classes. Your changes apply to all instances of the objects, so it's very easy to introduce conflicts or strange bugs in places you're not expecting them. This applies doubly for any code you plan to distribute in a library. People may not take kindly to libraries changing the global object prototypes, especially if it breaks their own code.

You won't be surprised to see that this operator translates directly to the object's `.prototype`:

```
Date.prototype.getYearAE = function() {
  var monthOffset;
  monthOffset = this.getMonth() < 11 ? 1 : 0;
  return this.getFullYear() - 1944 - monthOffset;
};
```

This flexible tool allows us to attach methods to the prototype and forgo the niceties of CoffeeScript class syntax if we so choose. All the power of JavaScript prototypes is still accessible; it's merely prettied up for the most common form of usage.

Constructors

When initializing a new object, we'll often find that we want to do some setup on the new object. This may include setting default values for properties, setting values for properties that are always required, or doing some additional computation before saving the results in the object's state.

So far, we've set properties on our objects *after* initializing them, like this:

```
plane = new Airplane()
plane.color = "white"
```

While it's nice to set properties this way some of the time, it becomes tiresome to do it all the time. It tends to move initialization logic out of the class and into the calling context, which leads to repetitive code. And if our caller makes a new object but forgets the subsequent initialization steps, we could end up in a weird half-initialized state, where things we expect to be present are not present.

The best way to deal with this is to define a constructor method. In CoffeeScript, this method is declared inside the class body, just like any other. It is identified as the constructor by being literally named `constructor`.

```
class Train
  constructor: (numCars, type="diesel") ->
    @type = type
    @numCars = numCars
    @load = 0
    @capacity = numCars * 100
  describe: ->
    "A #{@type} train with #{@numCars} cars." +
      " Current filled: #{@load}/#{@capacity} tons."

train = new Train(35)
console.log train.describe()
train2 = new Train 20, "steam"
console.log train2.describe()
```

We're defining a new `Train` class. The constructor takes two arguments, a required number of cars the train is pulling, and an optional type of train. You can see that this means `new Train` now accepts arguments. As with other method invocations in CoffeeScript, parentheses are optional here.

Our constructor stores the `numCars` and `type` values as properties of the object. It also does some additional work—it sets the current load (how much cargo the train is carrying) to 0, and it calculates how much cargo the train *can* carry based on the number of cars (estimating 100 tons of capacity per car).

There's one more nice feature CoffeeScript offers to help us pare down our constructor. The lines where we save constructor arguments to properties are very common and, in many cases, very repetitive:

```
constructor: (numCars, type="diesel") ->
    @type = type
    @numCars = numCars
```

If we use @ directly in the argument list, CoffeeScript will automatically assign the passed value to a property of the same name, allowing us to omit those lines:

```
constructor: (@numCars, @type="diesel") ->
    @load = 0
    @capacity = @numCars * 100
```

This version will work exactly the same and leaves us with a cleaner constructor. This technique is actually available in any object method, though there are not many reasons to use it outside of a constructor.

CoffeeScript constructors in JavaScript

Let's see how this constructor method we defined translates to JavaScript:

```
Train = (function() {
  function Train(numCars, type) {
    this.numCars = numCars;
    this.type = type != null ? type : "diesel";
    this.load = 0;
    this.capacity = this.numCars * 100;
  }

  Train.prototype.describe = function() {
    return ("A " + this.type + " train with " + this.numCars + "
cars.") + (" Current filled: " + this.load + "/" + this.capacity + "
tons.");
  };

  return Train;
})();
```

When we looked at our `Airplane` model, the inner named function was empty. This time, that named function is where we find our constructor code. This will be run when the object is instantiated, thanks to the mechanics of JavaScript's `new`.

Calling methods statically on classes

Most of the time we want the methods we attach to a class to be available on every instance of that class. In JavaScript, this means attaching them to the class prototype. Occasionally, though, we wish to attach a method to the class itself, so that it is always available from a single reference without instantiating any objects. These are commonly known as **static methods** or **class methods**. These types of method declarations are sometimes used to group many utility functions under a single namespace (think of the `Math` class in the standard JavaScript library). Let's build one of those.

```
class Bicycle
  @frameSizeByHeight = (riderHeight) ->
    Math.floor riderHeight * 0.82

for h in [60, 68, 72]
  console.log "A #{h}\" rider needs a size " +
    "#{Bicycle.frameSizeByHeight h} bike."
```

We have a `Bicycle` class. One common calculation related to bikes is determining what size bike someone needs given their height. It doesn't make sense for us to construct an instance of this class to do the calculation, since we might need it to know the size before we build a bike. By making this a static method on the `Bicycle` class, we can keep the code where it's relevant but have it always available. You can see we call it directly on the class, as `Bicycle.frameSizeByHeight`.

Another use for static methods is to build helpers that will find or create a new instance of a class when invoked. Let's build one of those now. There are many choices to make when building a bike; you can combine parts in many different ways. However, many people don't care about the details—they only want to choose what type of bike they are buying, like "road bike" or "mountain bike". We'll build a helper that accepts a type and sets up the details accordingly.

```
class Bicycle
  constructor: (@color, @size,
    @frameType, @tireWidth, @handlebarType) ->
    # Our constructor is empty for now

  @frameSizeByHeight = (riderHeight) ->
```

```
      Math.floor riderHeight * 0.82

  @buildPackageDeal = (color, type, riderHeight) ->
    basics = [color, @frameSizeByHeight(riderHeight)]
    details = switch type
      when "road"
        ["road", "23c", "drop bars"]
      when "commuter"
        ["road", "30c", "flat bars"]
      when "mountain"
        ["mountain", "2in", "flat bars"]
    args = basics.concat details
    new Bicycle(args...)

myBike = Bicycle.buildPackageDeal "black", "commuter", 66
```

You can see that our constructor accepts a number of arguments for details like tire width and handlebar style. Thanks to the helpful syntax for setting properties, we don't need to write anything in the body of the constructor.

Our `buildPackageDeal` helper only takes three arguments: the color, the type of bike, and the rider's height. We're calling the `frameSizeByHeight` utility that we wrote earlier to determine the frame size. Since we're invoking one static method from another, we can use @ to represent the class itself. We use a switch statement to set up the details of the bike, then combine them with the color and frame size to make arguments for the constructor.

This is another great time to use a splat when invoking a function. Even though it takes a set number of arguments, we want to construct our argument array dynamically. This helps us avoid repetitive code. Once we have built our argument list, we pass it to the constructor and return the new object. These sorts of methods allow us to keep repeated patterns in the class where they belong, while still offering flexible ways to build new objects.

We can also attach static properties to the class. This is useful when we have constants or other magical values that we want to keep associated with the class, but may wish to access without an instance:

```
class Bicycle
  @WHEELS = 2
  # ...

console.log "Bikes have #{Bicycle.WHEELS} wheels."
```

I like to name my constants with all capital letters. This is a nice convention that makes it clear that this value is not expected to change during execution.

Inheritance

Inheritance is a powerful concept that many modern programming languages use extensively. JavaScript has never embraced it wholeheartedly, in large part because implementing it has always been slightly awkward and error-prone due to some omissions in the JavaScript language. Thankfully, CoffeeScript patches up those holes and makes inheritance a first-class experience again.

Inheritance is used to define **is-a** relationships, such as "an Apple *is a* type of Fruit". Child classes (like Apple) inherit behavior from parent classes (like Fruit), while often adding more behavior or selectively modifying existing behavior. Inheritance can be chained through several generations, and a child inherits behavior from all of its ancestors, with priority given to the nearest. This is a powerful mechanism for code reuse, and is a good way to model many logical relationships.

Be cautious not to overuse inheritance. There are other ways to reuse code, so don't force inheritance onto a relationship that doesn't call for it. When in doubt, ask yourself if your child really *is a* kind of its parent, or if it holds some other relationship to the parent (such as **belongs-to** or **delegates-to**).

In CoffeeScript, we use `extends` in the class definition to show that this class inherits from another class.

```
class Automobile
  honk: ->
    console.log "Beep!"

class Hatchback extends Automobile

myCar = new Hatchback()
myCar.honk()
```

First, we define our `Automobile` class and give it a `honk` method, because we expect every car to have that ability. Then we define our `Hatchback` class and indicate that it extends `Automobile`. That's all we need to do; `Hatchback` will inherit the methods attached to `Automobile`, so we can call `honk()` on our new hatchback object and it will work.

Inherited methods are available to the rest of the class, just like normal:

```
class Hatchback extends Automobile
  carAlarm: ->
    @honk()
    @honk()
    @honk()

myCar = new Hatchback()
myCar.carAlarm()
```

We've given our hatchback an alarm that triggers the horn several times when it goes off (very annoying, just like a real car alarm). We are free to call the inherited @honk() just like we would call any other method attached to this object.

If we wish to override an inherited method, we simply declare the method again in the child class:

```
class Truck extends Automobile
  honk: ->
    console.log "BRAAAAAP"
```

Since truck horns are much louder than standard car horns, we've overridden honk() to produce a different noise here.

We can also override a method while retaining the behavior of the parent, by calling super:

```
class PoliceCar extends Automobile
  honk: ->
    super
    console.log "Wee-oo wee-oo wee-oo!"
```

Since police cars use their horn and a siren, we call super, which invokes the honk method we defined on Automobile. Then we add our own behavior, a siren noise.

When an inherited method takes arguments, we can invoke super in different ways for different results.

```
class Automobile
  radio: (volume=0) ->
    @radioVolume = volume
```

If we call `super` alone on the line, as we did before, it will call the parent's method *with all arguments that were passed in.*

```
class Truck extends Automobile
  radio: (volume) ->
    super
truck = new Truck
truck.radio 9 # "Radio at 9"
```

Calling `super` with arguments will pass *just those arguments*, ignoring any passed in.

```
class Truck extends Automobile
  radio: (volume) ->
    super volume + 2
truck = new Truck
truck.radio 9 # "Radio at 11"
```

And calling `super()` with parentheses makes it explicit that we wish to pass *no arguments*.

```
class Truck extends Automobile
  radio: (volume) ->
    super()
truck = new Truck
truck.radio 9 # "Radio at 0"
```

This gives us a lot of control and convenience when deciding how to call a parent method.

CoffeeScript's inheritance in JavaScript

Let's see what our inheritance relationship looks like in JavaScript. This part gets a little complicated, but it's worth working through — you might learn something new about both CoffeeScript and JavaScript!

Let's look at our `Hatchback` class:

```
Hatchback = (function(_super) {
  __extends(Hatchback, _super);

  function Hatchback() {
    _ref1 = Hatchback.__super__.constructor.apply(this, arguments);
    return _ref1;
  }
```

```
Hatchback.prototype.carAlarm = function() {
  this.honk();
  this.honk();
  return this.honk();
};

return Hatchback;

}) (Automobile);
```

Because inheritance isn't completely natural in JavaScript, CoffeeScript uses a couple of helpers to keep everything manageable. We'll find __extends defined at the very beginning of our JavaScript.

```
var __hasProp = {}.hasOwnProperty,
__extends = function(child, parent) {
  for (var key in parent) {
    if (__hasProp.call(parent, key))
      child[key] = parent[key];
  }
  function ctor() { this.constructor = child; }
  ctor.prototype = parent.prototype;
  child.prototype = new ctor();
  child.__super__ = parent.prototype;
  return child;
};
```

This function takes two arguments, a child and a parent (in our example, these are Hatchback and Automobile, respectively). First it transfers all of the parent's own properties (guarded by hasOwnProperty) to the child. Next, it creates a named function and uses it to build the appropriate prototype chain for our child class. Finally, it sets a special property on the child, __super__. This property isn't meant to be accessed directly, but will be used by CoffeeScript.

We saw how JavaScript's prototypes provide class-like behavior by making methods available to all instances of the class. As it turns out, they also help us provide inherited behavior. If a property or method isn't found in an object or the object's prototype, it will then check its *prototype's prototype*. That convoluted code in __extends is setting the parent prototype to the class we're inheriting from. This is how Hatchback is able to access the honk method—it doesn't find it in Hatchback.prototype, but it *does* find it in Automobile.protoype.

How do our calls to super work? We can get a hint by looking at the constructor:

```
function Hatchback() {
  _ref1 = Hatchback.__super__.constructor.apply(this, arguments);
  return _ref1;
}
```

Since we didn't define a constructor for this class ourselves, CoffeeScript has stepped in and created a one that delegates to the parent constructor. You can see that we're using the special __super__ property that was set by the __extends function.

This same property is used when we explicitly call super, such as the honk method of our PoliceCar class:

```
PoliceCar.prototype.honk = function() {
  PoliceCar.__super__.honk.apply(this, arguments);
  return console.log("Wee-oo wee-oo wee-oo!");
};
```

This also uses __super__ to call the parent's honk method (with any passed arguments) before executing this class' own code.

There you have it, the secrets of CoffeeScript's inheritance! We've learned that even though CoffeeScript classes have a different outward appearance, underneath they make heavy use of JavaScript's prototypes. A little extra code sits on top to correct some deficiencies in the plain JavaScript definition of classes, but that's the only extra complexity there is.

Using CoffeeScript with other class libraries

CoffeeScript classes are a great way to organize your code, and work just fine on their own. Sometimes, though, you'll be using a JavaScript framework that provides (among other things) its own class structures. It's usually possible to build these classes in CoffeeScript, but the exact mechanism will vary depending on the framework.

We'll look at two popular frameworks here. If you have another framework you wish to use, it's likely that it will fall into one of these two categories. In the first, we use the full CoffeeScript class system, and integrate it with the framework through standard JavaScript functionality. In the second, we use the framework's system to define classes, but still make use of syntactic CoffeeScript sugar when we're filling in the classes' behavior.

Backbone classes in CoffeeScript

Backbone.js is a popular JavaScript framework that offers models, collections, views, and a router. It has a lot in common philosophically with CoffeeScript—both projects believe in building on existing practices, leaving a small footprint, and working *with*, not *against* JavaScript. So it seems only right that CoffeeScript provides first-class support for Backbone classes.

Backbone provides helpers to accomplish some of the same things CoffeeScript provides. Here's the JavaScript version of defining a parent and child class in Backbone.

 All models in Backbone inherit important functionality from `Backbone.Model`.

```
var Note = Backbone.Model.extend({
  allowedToEdit: function(account) {
    return true;
  }
});

var PrivateNote = Note.extend({
  allowedToEdit: function(account) {
    return account.owns(this);
  }
});
```

Instead of using `Backbone.Model.extend` to define this class, we can declare it in standard CoffeeScript style:

```
class Note extends Backbone.Model
  allowedToEdit: (account) ->
    true

class PrivateNote extends Note
  allowedToEdit: (account) ->
    account.owns @
```

Our class will still work perfectly with Backbone! All the necessary Backbone functionality has been inherited, thanks to our `extends Backbone.Model`. We've reaped big benefits from the fact that CoffeeScript and Backbone both use the traditional best practices for JavaScript classes. Since we're working with full-fledged CoffeeScript classes, we also have access to niceties such as `super` if we need it.

CoffeeScript is also a natural fit for the rest of Backbone. For example, properties on Backbone classes are always accessed with `get` and `set` methods (this allows Backbone to fire events when the properties of a model change). CoffeeScript makes this smooth as butter:

```
class Sidebar extends Backbone.Model
  promptColor: ->
    cssColor = prompt "Please enter a CSS color:"
    @set color: cssColor
```

Using `@get` and `@set` makes the code wonderfully readable, and fits well with the rest of the class style.

There's one important difference to note about Backbone. In most cases, we will control the setup of a new object by defining an `initialize` method. This is where we'll set properties and do most other ordinary class setup. While we *can* override `constructor` in Backbone, we will usually only wish to do this if we want to control the behavior of the Backbone code itself.

Ember classes in CoffeeScript

Ember.js is a newer JavaScript framework that is gaining momentum quickly. It offers a lot of functionality, and intends to be the indispensable tool for serious client-side web development. While Ember does not integrate as tightly with CoffeeScript, there's still nothing preventing it from being a good experience.

While we are focusing on Ember in this section, the advice applies equally well to most other JavaScript frameworks. Even without custom-built support, using CoffeeScript to work with these frameworks should be seamless (remember, "It's just JavaScript!"), and you can still reap the benefits of cleaner, more readable, less error-prone code.

Here's an Ember model declaration in JavaScript:

```
App.Person = DS.Model.extend({
  firstName: DS.attr('string'),
  lastName: DS.attr('string'),

  fullName: function() {
    return this.get('firstName') +
           " " + this.get('lastName');
  }.property('firstName', 'lastName')
});
```

Here's the same declaration in CoffeeScript:

```
App.Person = DS.Model.extend
  firstName: DS.attr 'string'
  lastName: DS.attr 'string'

  fullName: (->
    "#{@get 'firstName'} #{@get 'lastName'}"
  ).property 'firstName', 'lastName'
```

This time, we're using Ember's `DS.Model.extend` to build our class instead of CoffeeScript's class syntax. Ember's classes depend on some more complicated functionality that isn't all inherited normally, so we'll go with the flow. This means we'll need to depend on the Ember utilities to handle issues like inheritance and super. We can use the `@get` and `@set` accessors again, just as we did in Backbone, and our code has benefited from the cleaner syntax.

> If you'd like an experience more customized to Ember, you could try the **EmberScript** project. EmberScript is a fork of CoffeeScript that is tailored specially to Ember development. It builds directly to Ember classes, and offers special syntax to control observable properties and other Ember constructs. While EmberScript is an actively maintained project, keep in mind that it *is* a different project with its own development cycle, and a small extra learning curve. You can find out more about EmberScript at http://emberscript.com/.

Summary

In this chapter, we learned all about classes in CoffeeScript. We saw:

- How to define and instantiate classes
- How to attach properties and methods to classes, and how to call them internally with `@`
- How to attach static properties and methods to the class object itself
- How to use constructors to perform initialization for the class
- How to use CoffeeScript classes in `Ember.js` and `Backbone.js`
- How CoffeeScript implements all this using JavaScript's prototype system

Now that we know almost everything there is to know about CoffeeScript classes, we're ready to put this knowledge into practice. The next chapter is going to be all about using classes to create modular, maintainable, understandable code. We're going to return to our pet shop application and do some serious refactoring.

6

Refactoring with Classes

In the previous chapter, we learned all about classes in CoffeeScript. Classes are a powerful organizational tool. They let us define objects to separate our code conceptually, and provide mechanisms for code sharing and state management to further enhance what we can do with them.

In this chapter, we'll be putting all this knowledge to work. We're returning to our pet shop application, and we'll be reworking most of the code. We will:

- Use classes to define the basic data structures of our application
- Use classes to define the display logic of our application
- Use static properties and methods to keep our code organized
- Use inheritance to reduce code duplication

The refactoring cycle

When I work on software projects, I like to perform frequent iterations of refactoring amongst periods of adding functionality. This tends to result in much higher-quality software: if I regularly set aside time for refactoring, I can catch any organizational problems before they grow out of control. Like tending a garden, weeds inevitably sprout up, and culling them is an unavoidable (and not entirely unpleasant) part of the job.

The other benefit of frequent refactoring iterations is that hindsight always outperforms foresight. Looking back on code I've already written makes it much easier to see what parts of the application may be a problem, and where I should devote some extra effort to code cleanup. Knowing that I will take the time to go over my code in the future frees me up from worrying about it in the present. Instead of agonizing over writing *perfect* code the first time I do it, I am happy to write *good-enough* code the first time, secure in the knowledge that I'll revisit it later and improve it if needed.

Our pet shop application isn't huge yet, but it has already become a little unwieldy. This is a perfect time for our first refactoring iteration.

Structuring our data with classes

Let's define a simple class to represent a person. Right now we only have one person represented in the project—the owner—but in the future we may have more people, such as employees. It will be helpful to have a class that encapsulates all the shared logic for dealing with people. We'll start out with a simple class:

```
class window.Person
  constructor: (@name) ->
```

Right now our class contains only a constructor. We learned in the previous chapter that putting `@name` in the constructor arguments automatically assigns it as a property of the new object.

We'll put this class in a new file, named `person.coffee`. Having each class in a separate file is a good convention to follow. Since classes naturally encapsulate shared pieces of logic, it's a good way to split things up; it keeps our code manageable while still making everything easy to find. Our `setup.coffee` was already getting a bit long, so moving some of the logic into classes will help shrink that file.

We've attached our class to the `window` object to make it global. If we had not done this, it wouldn't be accessible from `setup.coffee`, because CoffeeScript keeps everything in the local scope.

If you'd rather not have all classes in the global scope (or if you are building a library to distribute to others), you can namespace all your classes by attaching them to a single global object (which is traditionally named after your application). If we were to do this, we'd define a global object before the rest of our code:

```
PetShop ?= {}
```

Then we would define our classes as follows:

```
class PetShop.Person
    # ...
```

This minimizes scope pollution, and prevents possible class name conflicts. However, our app is fairly small and won't have any conflicts, so we'll leave everything in the global scope.

We need to include our new JavaScript file in `index.html`:

```
<script src="person.js"></script>
<script src="setup.js"></script>
```

Now in `setup.coffee`, we'll use our new class for the owner property:

```
shop = {
  owner: new Person "Ian"
  # …
}
```

Our new class is all ready, and if we reload the page, we should see the same heading as before.

Welcome to Ian's Pet Shop

Adding business logic

Our application will now work just like it did before we added the `Person` class. However, now that we have a class to organize our logic, it's very easy to add additional functionality without cluttering up the rest of our code. Let's fix a small bug in our formatting of the owner's name. We use this name to display a message like **Welcome to Ian's Pet Shop**. While this works well for my name, it gets the grammar wrong if we use a name like Jess. Since Jess ends with an "s", we should display **Jess' Pet Shop**, not **Jess's Pet Shop**. Let's add a method to our class to give the proper possessive form:

```
class window.Person
  constructor: (@name) ->

  possessiveName: ->
    if @name[@name.length - 1] in ['s', 'x', 'z']
      "#{@name}'"
    else
      "#{@name}'s"
```

Our `possessiveName` method checks the last letter of the `@name` property, and returns a different string if it's in the array of special letters. Now we can call this method on our owner object and replace the `'s` in several places in our code. In `setup.coffee`:

```
nameElement.innerHTML = shop.owner.possessiveName()
document.title = "#{shop.owner.possessiveName()} Pet Shop"
```

And in `index.html`:

```
<h1>Welcome to <span id="owner_name"></span> Pet Shop</h1>
```

Putting this logic in a class method means we can call it in as many places as we want without repeating the logic. This is great for writing clean and maintainable code.

If we reload our application, we can see our new, grammatically correct heading:

Welcome to Jess' Pet Shop

More data modeling

Now we'll define another class: `Animal`. This class will be the core of our application data, since our application spends most of its time dealing with animals. We'll start with the class constructor.

We *could* define a constructor that takes all the properties as arguments. However, the animals have a sizable number of properties, some of which are optional. So that would make for a slightly awkward constructor. Besides, we already have our data in a structured format—in our case it's a hard-coded array of objects, but in a full-fledged application it might be from a database or other storage medium. Let's build a helper to translate from our structured data format into a class instance.

We'll use a static method on our `Animal` class to do the work. This is one of the use cases we covered in the previous chapter. It keeps our helper tied to the `Animal` class, the most sensible place for it.

```
class window.Animal
  @fromHash: (data) ->
    animal = new @
    animal[key] = val for key, val of data
    animal
```

Our helper is very simple. It builds a new `Animal` and assigns all the values passed in as properties of the new object, then returns the new object. We can use this method to create new instances of the `Animal` class as follows:

```
fido = Animal.fromHash name: "Fido", type: "dog", age: 6
```

Let's add one more piece. We can build animals from our structured data objects, so now we'll write some code to loop through all our pet data and return an array of animals. We'll also move our data object into `animal.coffee`—that's a better place for it than `setup.coffee`. Let's add another static method to `Animal`:

```
  @loadSeedData: ->
    animalData = [
      name: "Kelsey"
      type: "dog"
      age: 2
      breed: "Labrador"
      description: "A sweet and loyal dog. Loves to play fetch.
Sometimes drinks out of the toilet."
    ,
      # ...the rest of the data
    ]
    for animal in animalData
      @fromHash animal
```

For each object in the array, we build a new class instance. Thanks to the `for` loop acting as an expression and CoffeeScript's implicit function returns, this is all we need to do for this function to return an array of `Animal` objects.

We're ready to start using our `Animal` class in the application. Remember to add it to `index.html`:

```
<script src="person.js"></script>
<script src="animal.js"></script>
<script src="setup.js"></script>
```

> Keeping track of all the JavaScript files can become a nuisance once you have many classes to deal with. If your application has a build process that uses a JavaScript minifier, you can set it to concatenate all your files first, so only one `<script>` tag is needed. Another solution is to use a module system such as **RequireJS** or **cujo.js**. These allow you to easily manage dependencies, and as a bonus will help you avoid polluting the global scope.

Our `setup.coffee` code becomes one simple line for the pets:

```
shop = {
  owner: new Person "Ian"
  animals: Animal.loadSeedData()
}
```

This file is now much easier to work with, and the seed data is easy to find if we ever wish to revisit it.

More business logic

Now that we've defined our `Animal` class, we can start refactoring our application code. Any logic that's closely tied to the `Animal` can be pulled into that class, and we'll be making use of the concepts we learned last chapter while we do it.

Let's start with our `animalBehaviors` function. We wrote this function in *Chapter 4, Improving Our Application*, to tell us what sound and action each pet made. Here's what it looks like right now, defined in `setup.coffee`:

```
animalBehaviors = (animal) ->
  switch animal.type
```

```
when "cat" then ["meow", null]
when "dog" then ["bark", "wag"]
when "rabbit" then [null, "hop hop"]
when "horse", "donkey"
    ["neigh", null]
else [null, null]
```

The name of the function, and the fact that it takes an `Animal` object as the only argument, are helpful signs that this might be a candidate for refactoring. Indeed, upon further inspection we can see that this logic is all animal-related logic. Let's move it to our class:

```
class window.Animal
  behaviors: ->
    switch @type
      when "cat" then ["meow", null]
      when "dog" then ["bark", "wag"]
      when "rabbit" then [null, "hop hop"]
      when "horse", "donkey"
        ["neigh", null]
      else [null, null]
```

We've shortened the method name to simply `behaviors`, since it no longer needs the clarification of what subject it deals with (being attached to the `Animal` class makes that clear). The method no longer takes an argument, because the animal in question is now `this`, the class instance it is called upon. Our switch statement uses `@type`. Remember, this is a shorthand for `this.type`, which references one of the properties we set in our `Animal.fromHash` helper.

Now we just need to update the call to this method, which is in `formatPetName`:

```
formatPetName = (pet, showBehavior) ->
  result = pet.name
  if showBehavior
    [sound, action] = pet.behaviors()
```

Instead of calling `animalBehaviors(pet)`, we can now call the method right on the pet object. Much simpler, and we have removed some code from `setup.coffee`.

Managing display logic with classes

Looking at `setup.coffee`, we can see that a lot of the remaining code deals with formatting HTML output. A lot of it is specific to displaying animal descriptions, so let's start with that. We could move these functions to the `Pet` class, but it's considered a best practice to separate the **business logic** of your application from the **display logic**. Mixing data operations with display output tends to create tightly coupled code, making it very difficult to make changes to either the backend or the frontend later on.

Instead, we'll separate this logic into **view** classes. These will concern themselves with displaying the page and responding to user input, but will leave any manipulation of the data to the other classes. We'll start with the view for a single pet. Let's create a new class in `pet_view.coffee`.

```
class window.PetView
  constructor: (@pet) ->
```

This class' constructor takes a single argument, a `Pet` object. It will obtain values from this object when building the output.

The first two functions we'll move into this class are `formatPetDescription` and `imageTag`:

```
class window.PetView
  constructor: (@pet) ->

  formattedDescription: ->
    "<h2>#{@pet.name}</h2>" +
      "<h3 class='breed'>#{@pet.breed} " +
      "(#{@pet.age ? "??"} years old)</h3>" +
      @imageTag(@pet.image) +
      "<p class='description'>#{@pet.description}</p>"

  imageTag: (filename) ->
    if filename?
      "<img src='images/#{filename}' />"
    else
      ""
```

These haven't changed too much. Instead of taking an argument, the dynamic values are now pulled from the `@pet` property. We can call `imageTag` from `formattedDescription` using `@` because it is also defined on this class.

Now we'll need to change the place where the description is used, inside the `selectPet` function in `setup.coffee`:

```coffee
window.selectPet = (petIndex, element) ->
  pet = shop.animals[petIndex]
  petView = new PetView pet
  petInfo = document.getElementById "pet_information"
  petInfo.innerHTML = petView.formattedDescription()
  # ...
```

We instantiate a new `PetView` object, passing the selected pet to the constructor. Then we ask the view for the formatted output to insert into our page.

We've got two more functions to move into this view: `formatPetLink`, and `formatPetName`.

```coffee
class window.PetView
  # ...
  formattedName: (showBehavior) ->
    result = @pet.name
    if showBehavior
      [sound, action] = @pet.behaviors()
      [behavior, cssClass] = if sound?
        ["#{sound}!", "sound"]
      else
        [action, "action"]

      result += " <span class='#{cssClass}'>#{behavior.
toLowerCase()}</span>"
    result

  formattedLink: (i, showBehavior=true) ->
    "<a href='#' onclick='selectPet(#{i}, this)'>" +
      "#{@formattedName showBehavior}</a>"
```

As before, we now reference properties of this view instead of taking the `pet` as an argument, but the logic is otherwise unchanged. We have two invocations to change in `setup.coffee`. The first is in `displayPetList`:

```coffee
window.displayPetList = (filter="All") ->
  petOutput = for pet, i in shop.animals when filter is "All" or
filter.toLowerCase() is pet.type
    petView = new PetView pet
    "<li>#{petView.formattedLink i}</li>"
```

The second is in `displayFeatured`:

```
displayFeatured = (featuredPets...) ->
  # ...
  chosenPetView = new PetView chosenPet
  featured.innerHTML = "<span class='title'>Featured Pet</span>" +
    chosenPetView.formattedLink fullListIndex, false
```

If you're thinking it's a little weird that we're instantiating this view a number of different times in different places, you're right. We'll deal with that soon.

Displaying a collection

We've still got quite a bit of view logic in `setup.coffee`. If we look through it, we can see that most of the remaining code deals with displaying a list of pets, and reacting when the user clicks on something related to that list. This doesn't fit well in `PetView`, which deals with displaying information for a single pet. Instead, we'll make a second view devoted to the list itself, in `pet_list_view.coffee`.

```
class window.PetListView
  constructor: (@views) ->
    # Nothing to do here
```

This view will take an array of `PetView` objects. Those objects are still responsible for rendering output for individual pets, but this new view will be responsible for the list itself and all behavior related to that.

First we'll move `displayPetList` from `setup.coffee` into this new view, and rename it:

```
class window.PetListView
  # ...
  renderList: (filter="All") ->
    petOutput = for view, i in @views when filter is "All" or filter.
toLowerCase() is view.pet.type
      "<li>#{view.formattedLink i}</li>"

    availablePets = document.getElementById("available_pets")
    availablePets.innerHTML = petOutput.join ""
```

The `for` loop now takes view objects out of this object's `@views` property. Because it's getting the view directly, it no longer needs to instantiate one itself, but may call `formattedLink` directly.

Next we'll move and rename `selectPet` and `displayFeatured`:

```
class window.PetListView
  # ...
  selectPet: (petIndex, element) ->
    petView = @views[petIndex]
    petInfo = document.getElementById "pet_information"
    petInfo.innerHTML = petView.formattedDescription()
    for link in document.querySelectorAll("#available_pets a")
      link.className = ""
    element.className = "selected"

  renderFeatured: (featuredPets...) ->
    chosenPetIndex = Math.floor Math.random() * featuredPets.length
    chosenPetName = featuredPets[chosenPetIndex]
    for view, i in @views when view.pet.name is chosenPetName
      [chosenPetView, fullListIndex] = [view, i]
    featured = document.getElementById("featured")
    featured.innerHTML = "<span class='title'>Featured Pet</span>" +
      chosenPetView.formattedLink fullListIndex, false
```

These methods have also been modified to use the `@views` property. Now the views can be instantiated once and used all over.

We also need to move the code that displays the featured pet box. This wasn't in a method yet, but now is a good time to put it in one:

```
renderFilteringBar: ->
  filteringOutput = for type in ["All", "Dog", "Cat", "Rabbit",
"Horse"]
    "<li><a href='#' onclick='displayPetList(\"#{type}\")'>#{type}</
a></li>"

  filteringOpts = document.getElementById("filtering_opts")
  filteringOpts.innerHTML = filteringOutput.join ""
```

We've got methods to render all the pieces of our pet list, so now we just need to tie it together with some initialization. We'll add a `render` method to our view:

```
render: ->
  @renderList()
  @renderFilteringBar()
  @renderFeatured "Chupa", "Kelsey", "Flops"
  window.listView = @
```

```
        window.displayPetList = (filterType) ->
          window.listView.renderList(filterType)
        window.selectPet = (index, element) ->
          window.listView.selectPet(index, element)
```

This calls each of our rendering methods to load the page. It also saves the view object to a global reference and creates global callbacks to invoke `renderList` and `selectPet`. These will be called just as they were before, to re-render some sections of the page when a user clicks on a pet link or the filtering options.

Now all we need to do is initialize our view in `setup.coffee`:

```
    petViews = (new PetView pet for pet in shop.animals)
    petListView = new PetListView petViews
    petListView.render()
```

We're building an array of `PetView` objects out of our pet arrays, then passing that array to the `PetViewList` constructor. Once we're ready to display our page, we call `render()`, which in turn performs all the necessary display work in our views.

The top-level display logic

We've drastically pared down the size of `setup.coffee`, which is great news. Now that it's so clean, it's easy to see the one remaining piece of view logic—it sticks out like a sore thumb!

```
    nameElement = document.getElementById("owner_name")
    nameElement.innerHTML = shop.owner.name
    document.title = "#{shop.owner.name}'s Pet Shop"
```

This doesn't really fit into either of the views we've built so far. It concerns the shop page as a whole—what's sometimes referred to as the **layout**. We'll create a new view to handle this, named `shop_view.coffee`.

```
    class window.ShopView
      constructor: (@owner, @mainContent) ->
      render: ->
        nameElement = document.getElementById("owner_name")
        nameElement.innerHTML = @owner.possessiveName()
        document.title = "#{@owner.possessiveName()} Pet Shop"
        @mainContent.render()
```

This view, like our `PetListView`, also implements a `render` method. Besides handling the page titles, this view is really the top-level arbiter of display logic. It's in charge of the page as a whole. Because of this, we're also giving it control of the rest of the page rendering. It takes another view, `@mainContent`, as an argument to the constructor, and it will call that view's `render` from within its own `render` method. We'll modify `setup.coffee` slightly to use this new arrangement:

```
petViews = (new PetView pet for pet in shop.animals)
petListView = new PetListView petViews
mainView = new ShopView shop.owner, petListView
mainView.render()
```

Now we only call `render` once from our setup code, and every view is responsible for the views it contains. Our `setup.coffee` is doing very little, which is exactly what we want. It sets things up and puts everything in the right places, but all the heavy lifting will take place in our other classes.

 We've just implemented a loose interpretation of a popular organizational scheme for web applications, **Model-View-Controller** (**MVC**). Most popular frontend JavaScript frameworks use this pattern, or its variant, **Model-View-ViewModel** (don't ask). The specifics vary by framework, but everything we've done here—separating display logic from data manipulations, putting the bulk of the code in classes with a thin layer of glue to coordinate everything—will feel familiar when you encounter it elsewhere.

Now we just need to add our new classes to the files included by `index.html`:

```html
<script src="pet_view.js"></script>
<script src="pet_list_view.js"></script>
<script src="shop_view.js"></script>
<script src="setup.js"></script>
```

Our new views should be working. Try out the application and see for yourself!

A final refactoring pass

Now that we've separated our logic and we have a feel for how it all fits together, let's take one more pass through our code looking for things that are out of place. Our first stop is this line, from `PetListView#render`:

```
@renderFeatured "Chupa", "Kelsey", "Flops"
```

The view shouldn't be concerned with the specific pets that are featured. Let's move this out of the view. Our controller (`setup.coffee`) is a pretty good place for this information. We'll add it to the data object there, and pass it to the `PetListView`:

```
shop = {
  owner: new Person "Ian"
  animals: Animal.loadSeedData()
  featured: [ "Chupa", "Kelsey", "Flops" ]
}
petViews = (new PetView pet for pet in shop.animals)
petListView = new PetListView petViews, shop.featured
mainView = new ShopView shop.owner, petListView
mainView.render()
```

Now we'll update `PetListView` to use this new argument:

```
class window.PetListView
  constructor: (@views, featuredPets) ->
    @featured = featuredPets
  render: ->
    @renderList()
    @renderFilteringBar()
    @renderFeatured()
    # ...
  renderFeatured: ->
    return unless @featured?
    chosenPetIndex = Math.floor Math.random() * @featured.length
    chosenPetName = @featured[chosenPetIndex]
    # ...
```

Our `renderFeatured` method now takes no arguments, and instead checks the `@featured` property set by the constructor. If `@featured` is present, it renders the featured page element.

Another line that could use some work is this one, from `PetListView#renderList`:

```
petOutput = for view, i in @views when filter is "All" or filter.
toLowerCase() is view.pet.type.
```

It's a long line and a bit hard to understand, which is a red flag that we should examine closer. Most of the logic here deals with the filtering options. The filtering behavior itself is part of the list view's responsibilities, but it shouldn't be expected to know about the actual filtering categories, or how to match a category against an animal.

We'll shift this responsibility to the `Animal` class:

```
class window.Animal
  # ...
  matchesFilter: (criteria) ->
    criteria is "All" or criteria.toLowerCase() is @type
```

Now we can simply call this method on an animal, passing the category, and receive a boolean indicating whether this object matches the filter criteria or not. This simplifies our loop:

```
renderList: (filter="All") ->
  petOutput =
    for view, i in @views when view.pet.matchesFilter filter
      # ...
```

Now that we've started pulling out the filtering logic, it seems clear that the list view shouldn't even need to know the specific category names. Those too can be shifted to the `Animal` class. We'll start by removing the default argument on `renderList`. If it receives a null value, it will pass that right through to `matchesFilter`, which can decide how to handle it.

```
renderList: (filter) ->
  # ...
```

We'll update `matchesFilter` to accommodate this change with a default argument value:

```
matchesFilter: (criteria="All") ->
  criteria is "All" or criteria.toLowerCase() is @type
```

We'll make one more change to finish removing the filtering logic from our view. All possible values for the filter are defined in `renderFilteringBar`:

```
renderFilteringBar: ->
  filteringOutput =
    for type in ["All", "Dog", "Cat", "Rabbit", "Horse"]
      # ...
```

This, too, can be moved to `Animal`. Since it is a value that pertains to the `Animal` class in general rather than a specific instance of the class, we'll attach it as a static property:

```
class window.Animal
  @CATEGORIES = ["All", "Dog", "Cat", "Rabbit", "Horse"]
  # ...
```

Now we'll update our view to use that static property:

```
renderFilteringBar: ->
  filteringOutput = for type in Animal.CATEGORIES
    # ...
```

There! We've pulled some logic out of the view and put it in much more sensible places in our `Animal` model. It will be easier to find and update in the future, and the view can concentrate on what it does best: display logic.

Using inheritance while refactoring

There's one more bit of refactoring that will help us pare down our code. We've got a pattern that's repeated in a number of places in our views:

```
availablePets = document.getElementById "available_pets"
availablePets.innerHTML = petOutput.join ""
```

We find a DOM element using an id, and then insert some generated output into it. It would be nice if we could encapsulate this logic somewhere. It will save us time, make our code easier to read, and if we want to change the pattern (say, to support older browsers), we'll only need to do it in one place.

This is a generic piece of display functionality, but we don't have a good way to share among all our view classes. Well… we *do* have a good way, we just haven't written it yet! This is a perfect situation for inheritance. We'll define a generic `View` class that all our views inherit from, which will give us an easy way to promote code reuse.

First add it to `index.html`, *before* the other view files:

```
<script src="view.js"></script>
<script src="pet_view.js"></script><!-- … -->
```

Then define our class in `view.coffee`:

```
class window.View
```

And update each of our view classes to inherit from `View`:

```
class window.ShopView extends View
  # ...
class window.PetListView extends View
  # ...
class window.PetView extends View
  # ...
```

Now that we have our `View` class defined, we can add a method in `view.coffee` to handle inserting rendered content into the page.

```
class window.View
  renderToElement: (id, output) ->
    el = document.getElementById(id)
    el.innerHTML = output
```

Now we're ready to use this. It's as easy as calling `@renderToElement` within our other class methods. Thanks to CoffeeScript setting the prototype chain correctly, these calls will bubble up to the definition in `View`.

Here's `ShopView`:

```
class window.ShopView extends View
  render: ->
    @renderToElement "owner_name", @owner.possessiveName()
    # ...
```

And here's `PetListView`:

```
class window.PetListView extends View
  renderList: (filter) ->
    # ...
    @renderToElement "available_pets", petOutput.join ""

  selectPet: (petIndex, element) ->
    petView = @views[petIndex]
    @renderToElement "pet_information", petView.formattedDescription()
    # ...

  renderFeatured: ->
    # ...
    @renderToElement "featured",
      "<span class='title'>Featured Pet</span>" +
      chosenPetView.formattedLink fullListIndex, false

  renderFilteringBar: ->
    # ...
    @renderToElement "filtering_opts", filteringOutput.join ""
```

Lovely! That's a lot of repetitive code cleaned up.

Now that we have this inheritance relationship defined, we'll also move the `imageTag` helper that was previously in `PetView` into our `View` class. We don't need to share that code yet, but it's clearly a generic method and fits best in the generic view class:

```
class window.View
  imageTag: (filename) ->
    if filename?
      "<img src='images/#{filename}' />"
    else
      ""
```

After adding this method to `View`, we can remove it from `PetView`. We don't need to change anything else about `PetView`. Thanks to inheritance, the call to `@imageTag` will work the same as always.

Getting the green light

Let's take a moment to test out our application and make sure everything is still working like before. The goal of refactoring is to clean up code problems without altering the behavior of the application. Try out the features we've built so far and make sure everything is working. If so, congratulations! You've successfully completed this project's first big refactoring!

Summary

Our application looks outwardly much the same as it did at the beginning of this chapter. Our code, on the other hand, does not. Classes helped us massively refactor and reorganize our codebase. We've achieved a much better separation of concerns, got rid of some repetitive code, and put all our methods in the logical places. We:

- Used model classes to represent the data and business logic of our application
- Used view classes to handle the display logic and user input
- Used inheritance and composition to share logic between classes

Now that our application is lean and mean, we're ready to add some more improvements. In the next chapter, we'll be learning about some advanced features of CoffeeScript. We'll learn new ways to manipulate different types of data, including our new classes. We'll also learn some common idioms that make your life easier and your code more powerful.

7
Advanced CoffeeScript Usage

We spent the previous chapter overhauling our application to be more modular and use classes. Now it's time to dig even deeper into CoffeeScript. In this chapter, we'll be looking at some advanced features of the language as well as some ways to use what we already know to write better, cleaner, and more powerful code. Think of this chapter as the gateway to becoming a CoffeeScript power user. We will:

- Learn about the subtleties of context when invoking methods on objects
- Learn an incredibly easy way to avoid repeating expensive operations by saving results in object state
- Learn a helpful idiom for passing lots of options to a function

Getting our context right

Now that we're starting to deal with classes a lot in our application, it's only a matter of time before we run into problems with context. When dealing with standalone functions, it's fairly easy to understand what data the function body sees. It knows about globals, variables defined within the function, and any variables that were present in the local scope when the function was defined. When methods are attached to objects, the question becomes a little more complicated. We'll look at one of the common sources of problems with object methods, and then we'll see how CoffeeScript can help us.

Let's make a simple class:

```
class Boat
  liftAnchor: (doneCallback) ->
    console.log "Lifting anchor."
  setSpeed: (speed) ->
    console.log "Adjusting speed to #{speed} knots."
  depart: ->
    @liftAnchor()
    @setSpeed 10
```

This works great if we wish to depart immediately:

```
caravel = new Boat
caravel.depart()
```

However, raising the anchor doesn't happen immediately. We should wait until the anchor is fully raised before getting under steam. We can do this without blocking by passing a callback to liftAnchor. This method knows how long it takes to raise the anchor, and will call the callback once it is finished.

```
liftAnchor: (doneCallback) ->
  console.log "Lifting anchor."
  if doneCallback?
    setTimeout doneCallback, 1000
```

You'll notice that we're only invoking the callback if it exists. This way, a caller who doesn't care about waiting for the anchor to finish raising may pass no arguments. We do care, so we will rearrange the calls in depart:

```
depart: ->
  @liftAnchor ->
    @setSpeed 10
```

We are now invoking setSpeed *inside* the callback passed to liftAnchor. This ensures that we won't try to get moving until the anchor is fully raised.

This looks good, but if we try to run the code, we get an error that the setSpeed function does not exist! What happened? JavaScript sets the value of this based on the way the method is invoked. When we invoke caravel.depart, the value of this is bound to the boat object. But when we invoke doneCallback, it isn't being called on an object, so this is bound to the global context. That is usually not what we want!

Another symptom of this problem is that even though functions are first-class objects, `caravel.depart()` does not behave the same as `func = caravel.depart; func()`.

Because our callback is invoked by the timeout with `this` bound to the global context, `@setSpeed` doesn't exist, and we get an error. What we want is to make sure that `this` is always bound to the boat instance inside the body of the callback. Luckily, CoffeeScript has a feature for precisely that. Declare a function with a fat arrow (`=>` instead of `->`). The function will now have `this` bound to the context in which it was declared.

```
depart: ->
  @liftAnchor =>
    @setSpeed 10
```

Now our delayed departure can take place without a hitch.

```
class Boat
  liftAnchor: (doneCallback) ->
    console.log "Lifting anchor."
    if doneCallback?
      setTimeout doneCallback, 1000
  setSpeed: (speed) ->
    console.log "Adjusting speed to #{speed} knots."
  depart: ->
    @liftAnchor =>
      @setSpeed 10

caravel = new Boat
caravel.depart()
```

Let's take a look at the JavaScript to see how CoffeeScript accomplishes the fat arrow binding.

```
Boat.prototype.depart = function() {
  var _this = this;
  return this.liftAnchor(function() {
    return _this.setSpeed(10);
  });
};
```

Before declaring the callback, it sets a local variable, _this, which simply references this. Even though the callback has a dynamically bound value of this, it still carries the local context in which it was declared, so the local variable _this won't change (a characteristic known as a **closure**). In the callback body, CoffeeScript substitutes _this to get access to the desired context. As usual, CoffeeScript is mimicking code a JavaScript developer might write by hand. Many JavaScript projects use a very similar technique, conventionally substituting a local variable named self for this.

> Since binding this is a common problem in JavaScript, especially when a class system is in use, other frameworks sometimes provide utilities that do a similar binding of this. For example, **Underscore.js** offers bind and bindAll. Even if you're using Underscore in your CoffeeScript project, though, there's little reason not to use the CoffeeScript syntax for all function bindings. It's concise and efficient.

You might wonder why we don't use fat arrows all the time. After all, couldn't we bind *every* method to the object context and save ourselves the trouble of worrying about it? Well, technically we could, but skinny arrows offer far better memory usage. A function declared with a skinny arrow exists only once in memory, while a function declared with a fat arrow exists once in memory for every different context. If you have many instances of a class, this adds up to a lot of wasted memory. Thus it's best to only use fat arrows when they're needed. You'll find that after a little practice, you'll get pretty good at anticipating when a fat arrow will be needed.

Using fat arrows in our project

We have already encountered a situation where we needed fat arrows — we just didn't know it yet! When we built our PetListView, we needed to declare a couple callback methods for click events. Since we needed these callbacks to invoke methods on our view, we stored a global reference to the view and referred back to it in the callbacks:

```
render: ->
  @renderList()
  @renderFilteringBar()
  @renderFeatured()
  window.listView = @
  window.displayPetList = (filterType) ->
    window.listView.renderList(filterType)
  window.selectPet = (index, element) ->
    window.listView.selectPet(index, element)
```

Global references are usually a **code smell**. They are fragile, difficult to manage, and tend to muddle the determinism of our code. And indeed, the use of a global here is a good hint to show us that we can improve our code. We don't *need* the global, we just need a way to call methods on our object. This is exactly what fat arrows do well!

```
render: ->
  @renderList()
  @renderFilteringBar()
  @renderFeatured()
  window.displayPetList = (filterType) =>
    @renderList(filterType)
  window.selectPet = (index, element) =>
    @selectPet(index, element)
```

Since this is now bound to our view object in the callbacks, we can call `@renderList` and `@selectPet` like normal method calls. We were able to get rid of the global reference completely and make our code more understandable to boot!

Saving our work with memoization

We're going to look at a simple technique we can use to avoid repeating work. This does not take the place of more advanced performance optimization, but it is a nice way to do some common-sense improvement with almost no effort on your part. The general idea, known as **memoization**, is to store calculated information so that we can quickly look it up later rather than recalculating it. Now that our application is using classes, we are dealing with objects, and objects have state that we can exploit to easily store modest amounts of data.

There are more complicated (and powerful) ways to memoize data, but we're going to keep it simple. When a piece of information is requested, we'll see if it's stored. If so, we return it immediately. If not, we calculate it and store the answer for later use. This technique is most helpful when we need to do some resource-intensive computation to receive an answer, or when we must use a slow channel such as network requests to retrieve information.

```
class Rocket
  getTrajectory: ->
    @trajectory ?= @doComplicatedMath()
```

That's it! The trajectory calculations will take place the first time the information is requested, and the stored value will be used from then on. We're getting some help from `?=`, which will only evaluate the right-hand side of the expression if `@trajectory` is null. We're also getting some help from CoffeeScript's implicit function returns. This method returns the result of the expression, which is the value of `@trajectory`, whether it was previously stored or just calculated.

We can also use a data structure to store more than one value:

```
class SecurityGate
  hasAccess: (guard) ->
    @access ?= {}
    @access[guard.badge_number] ?= checkCredentials guard.badge_number
```

This object remembers the result for every guard who has requested access. We just need something unique, such as a badge number, to use as a key in our memoized object.

> Make sure to only memoize information that won't change over the course of program execution. If you have information that will change over time or when data is updated, you need a **caching** solution instead.

Using memoization in our application

Our application isn't doing any serious heavy lifting or high-latency requests yet, so we don't have a perfect candidate to memoize. However, there is at least one method that's doing more than it needs. Let's look at `PetListView#renderFeatured`:

```
renderFeatured: ->
  return unless @featured?
  chosenPetIndex = Math.floor Math.random() * @featured.length
  chosenPetName = @featured[chosenPetIndex]
  for view, i in @views when view.pet.name is chosenPetName
    [chosenPetView, fullListIndex] = [view, i]
  @renderToElement "featured",
    "<span class='title'>Featured Pet</span>" +
    chosenPetView.formattedLink fullListIndex, false
```

Every time this method is called, it recalculates a random index to find the information for a featured pet. We can memoize this information since the featured pet shouldn't change over the program's execution (a single visitor's time on our site). We'll also be making our method **idempotent**, meaning we can call it as many times as we like and the result won't change.

Let's memoize the random index:

```
renderFeatured: ->
  return unless @featured?
  @chosenPetIndex ?= Math.floor Math.random() * @featured.length
  chosenPetName = @featured[@chosenPetIndex]
  for view, i in @views when view.pet.name is chosenPetName
```

```
        [chosenPetView, fullListIndex] = [view, i]
    @renderToElement "featured",
        "<span class='title'>Featured Pet</span>" +
        chosenPetView.formattedLink fullListIndex, false
```

That was pretty easy: just change the variable to a property of this object. But we don't need to stop there. Almost all the logic here is dependent on that index. If the index doesn't change, the rest of the values won't either. We can execute *most* of the code only the first time:

```
    renderFeatured: ->
      return unless @featured?
      unless @chosenPetView? and @fullListIndex?
        chosenPetIndex = Math.floor Math.random() * @featured.length
        chosenPetName = @featured[chosenPetIndex]
        for view, i in @views when view.pet.name is chosenPetName
          [@chosenPetView, @fullListIndex] = [view, i]
      @renderToElement "featured",
        "<span class='title'>Featured Pet</span>" +
        @chosenPetView.formattedLink @fullListIndex, false
```

This time we're memoizing `chosenPetView` and `fullListIndex`, because those are the final values used to render the element.

There's one more way we can approach this. This is more of a stylistic change, and you can decide if you like it more or less than the previous technique. Instead of an `if` block, we'll once again use `?=`, but include an entire block of code to execute if the value is `null`. To help, we'll use a special keyword, `do`. This keyword immediately executes a function it is given.

```
    renderFeatured: ->
      return unless @featured?
      @chosenFeatured ?= do =>
        chosenPetIndex = Math.floor Math.random() * @featured.length
        chosenPetName = @featured[chosenPetIndex]
        for view, i in @views when view.pet.name is chosenPetName
          return [view, i]
      [chosenPetView, fullListIndex] = @chosenFeatured
      @renderToElement "featured",
        "<span class='title'>Featured Pet</span>" +
        chosenPetView.formattedLink fullListIndex, false
```

We're now memoizing a **duple** (a two-element array) with the values we're interested in. If it does not exist, we use `do` to execute a function to calculate it. It's important that we use the fat arrow to define our function, since the body calls several object properties that need the correct context for `this`.

A new idiom: options objects

Now we're going to look at an idiom for passing options to a function. This isn't a new feature of CoffeeScript. Instead, it's a convention that makes use of several CoffeeScript features we've already learned, and uses them in a pattern that is easy to understand and useful in a wide variety of situations.

 This idiom is also common in Ruby programs. Ruby makes extensive use of **hashes** (the equivalent of simple objects), and has loose syntax rules (much like CoffeeScript) allowing hashes to be passed to functions without extra noise. Other languages, such as Python, offer similar benefits via **named arguments**.

The idea is simple: a function accepts an `options` object, which may contain keys for any less-common or less-obvious function arguments. This makes the options easier to understand from the code calling the function because there are keys to identify what each value does. It also alleviates the problems of keeping track of arguments and argument order, since object keys are not order-dependent and may be omitted if not needed.

This pattern is used occasionally in vanilla JavaScript libraries (such as jQuery's AJAX functions), but we can leverage the power of CoffeeScript to make it even more useful, and as a result use it in more places. We'll draw on a number of CoffeeScript features from the previous chapters to make options objects easier to define, easier to call, and easier to read.

First, we'll use optional arguments to default to an empty argument. This way the caller can omit the options entirely if no special values are needed.

```
launchSpaceship = (name, options={}) ->
  return if options.dryRun
  fireEngines()
```

Next, we'll use `?=` to fill in option values that we wish to have a special default:

```
launchSpaceship = (name, options={}) ->
  options.countdown ?= 10
  console.log "#{i}..." for i in [options.countdown..0]
  return if options.dryRun
  fireEngines()
```

We can always use the `?` operator as a shorthand default for a value that's only used in one place:

```
launchSpaceship = (name, options={}) ->
  checkFuel(options.expectedFuel ? 100)
```

```
options.countdown ?= 10
console.log "#{i}..." for i in [options.countdown..0]
return if options.dryRun
fireEngines()
```

Another common way to provide defaults for an object is to create a second object of default values and merge the two objects. Unfortunately, merging objects is not entirely trivial in JavaScript. You can do it naively with a CoffeeScript loop comprehension. This will work on vanilla, non-nested objects, but beware of using it on anything more complex.

```
options[k] ?= defaults[k] for k, v of defaults
```

Some JavaScript libraries include utility functions to merge objects. jQuery provides $.extend, and Underscore.js provides both _.extend and the more specialized _.defaults.

Now that we've defined this argument, CoffeeScript's permissive syntax means that we can pass our options to the function without braces, giving our function calls a very natural feel.

```
launchSpaceship "X900 Prototype", dryRun: true, countdown: 18
```

The options argument, by convention, should be the last argument the function accepts. One exception: if a function accepts a callback argument (common in asynchronous operations), the callback argument comes at the end, after options. In this case, you'll need to handle the default argument yourself. Still, I prefer to continue using the default argument notation for clarity.

```
fetchCatPhotos = (count, options={}, callback) ->
  # If only two arguments given, last argument is callback
  [options, callback] = [{}, options] unless callback?
  # Fetch cat photos
  callback photos
```

Using options objects in our application

Now that we've seen how options objects can make function signatures simpler, let's put them to use. We'll add a new feature to our app; we've decided to add a small thumbnail image to the **Featured Pet** section for any pet that has a photo available. Let's make some changes to our code to make this possible.

First we'll save new copies of our pet photos, resized to 50px. We'll use a naming scheme of `filename-size.ext` to track the different copies of our photos. So our new thumbnail files will be named `flops-thumb.jpg` and `chupa-thumb.jpg`. We'll also rename the existing full-sized photos to fit this scheme. They will now be `flops-original.jpg` and `chupa-original.jpg`.

Now we'll need to modify the `imageTag` method we are using to generate the HTML for an image. We'll let this method take an options object, with a `size` key that specifies the desired size of the image tag, either `original` or `thumb`.

> Passing the size as a separate argument keeps the specifics of our file naming scheme out of the rest of our application code. This way, if we later wish to change our image naming scheme from `images/flops-thumb.jpg` to, say, `images/thumbs/flops.jpg`, we will only need to change the code in one place rather than every place an image tag is created.

```coffeescript
imageTag: (filename, options={}) ->
  options.size ?= "original"
  if filename?
    sizedFilename = filename.replace /\.(jpg|png)$/, "-#{options.size}.$1"
    "<img src='images/#{sizedFilename}' />"
  else
    ""
```

Just like we saw with our previous examples, we are using an optional argument that the caller may omit to receive default values. If `size` is not set, we default it to `original`. Then, before creating the `img` tag, if the filename ends with `.jpg` or `.png` we add a `-size` suffix before the file extension to get the desired image. Because we set up our defaults carefully, our existing calls to this method will continue to work without modification.

Now that our image tag method can handle different image sizes, we need to update our `PetView` with the ability to put a thumbnail before the pet's name. Previously, we had set up the `formattedName` method to take a `showBehavior` argument that controls the animal sounds we print in the main list. Rather than adding another argument to the list, let's give `formattedName` an options object that will control the display of both the thumbnail and animal behavior.

```coffeescript
formattedName: (options={}) ->
  result = @pet.name
```

```
if options.showThumbnail
  result = imageTag(@pet.image, size: "thumb") + result

if options.showBehavior
  [sound, action] = @pet.behaviors()
  [behavior, cssClass] = if sound?
    ["#{sound}!", "sound"]
  else
    [action, "action"]

  result += " <span class='#{cssClass}'>#{
    behavior.toLowerCase()}</span>"
result
```

We've moved the `showBehavior` argument to a key in the options object, and added a new key, `showThumbnail`. If `showThumbnail` is enabled, we add an image tag using our newly-created `size` option.

We'll also update the method signature of `formattedLink`, which passes its options along to `formattedName`:

```
formattedLink: (i, options={}) ->
  "<a href='#' onclick='selectPet(#{i}, this)'>" +
    "#{@formattedName options}</a>"
```

Another benefit of using an options object is that future additions won't require any more changes to `formattedLink`'s arguments. It can pass the options object through to `formattedName` without caring too much about the contents. If every option was a separate argument, we'd need to continue updating `formattedLink` every time we added an option to `formattedName`.

Since we *did* change the method signatures with this options object, we'll need to update the places in our code that call these methods. The first is `PetListView#renderList`, which is responsible for the links in the main list of pets. These links should have a behavior, but no thumbnail.

```
renderList: (filter) ->
  petOutput = for view, i in @views when view.pet.matchesFilter
filter
    "<li>#{view.formattedLink I, showBehavior: true}</li>"
  @renderToElement "available_pets", petOutput.join ""
```

Now it's time to enable thumbnails in our featured pet display. We'll simply turn on the option in `renderFeatured`. These links should have a thumbnail, but no behavior.

```
renderFeatured: ->
  # ...
  @renderToElement "featured",
    "<span class='title'>Featured Pet</span>" +
    chosenPetView.formattedLink fullListIndex, showThumbnail: true
```

We'll also add a little CSS to `style.css` to format this thumbnail:

```
#featured img {
  margin-right: 0.5em;
}
```

We're ready! Reload our app and if the featured pet is one with a photo available, we should see a thumbnail beside it.

Looks great! We've added a nice new feature to the website, and we haven't unduly complicated our method signatures in the process.

Our options object makes it very easy to toggle flags on and off. For curiosity's sake, we can try rendering thumbnails in the main pet list as well, just by turning on the option in `renderList`:

```
renderList: (filter) ->
  petOutput = for view, i in @views when view.pet.matchesFilter
filter
      "<li>#{view.formattedLink i, showBehavior: true, showThumbnail:
true}</li>"
  @renderToElement "available_pets", petOutput.join ""
```

As easy as that, we have images in our main list:

Kelsey *"bark!"*

Sgt. Snuffles *"bark!"*

Chomps **hop hop**

 **Flops** **hop hop**

Bopper **hop hop**

Chairman Meow *"meow!"*

Jacques *"meow!"*

Chupa *"meow!"*

Alfred *"neigh!"*

I think it makes the page a little too busy, so we won't keep that option turned on. Still, it's nice to have the flexibility to try out new ideas. When it only takes a couple minutes to have a working prototype of an idea, we're free to try a number of things and not feel like we've wasted time if they don't work out.

Summary

In this chapter, we learned:

- How the value of this can change in a method body, and how to use fat arrows to get the behavior we want.

- How to use memoization to save and retrieve the results of expensive computation rather than repeating it.

- How to use options objects to clean up our method signatures and easily set defaults.

This chapter was a graduation of sorts. You're now extremely well-versed in the CoffeeScript language! You've learned almost all of the syntax, including some fairly advanced tools and tricks. The next few chapters are all about using CoffeeScript to accomplish *more, better*. First up is a very common paradigm in web development: dealing with asynchronous operations.

8
Going Asynchronous

Asynchronous operations are an important part of JavaScript application development, for both server-side and client-side code. It's time to dig in and learn what exactly they are, how they work, when they might surprise us, and how CoffeeScript can help us make the best of it.

We will:

- Understand what makes asynchronous operations special
- Fetch information from a remote API to use in our application
- Make multiple requests to the API at the same time
- Use a third-party library to make these requests easier

Understanding asynchronous operations

It's a word you've probably heard before, but may not understand exactly what it means or why we care. **Asynchronous** operations are operations that do not **block** while completing. What does that mean, exactly? Well, **synchronous** operations (the vast majority of commands in a program) get executed one at a time, in order. Consider this code:

```
mixBatter()
bakeCake()
frostCake()
```

Each of these functions is invoked in order, and not until the previous function returns. bakeCake is only invoked after mixBatter returns, and frostCake is invoked only after bakeCake returns. If bakeCake takes 40 minutes to return, well, frostCake will have to wait 40 minutes before it can run. We could say that bakeCake **blocks** execution until it is finished.

This makes the code very easy to reason about, and most of the time it's the behavior that we want. However, there are times where we might wish to start an operation but not wait for it to finish before doing more work. Most often, this is the case with various types of I/O, like reading from a hard disk, or making an HTTP request. Most I/O is much slower than a CPU, so if the whole program has to wait for the operation to finish, the CPU is sitting idle when it could be doing other important work.

The solution to this is to perform some operations **asynchronously**. This means that we will start the operation, but we won't wait for it to finish before we move on to other work. We can get important work done in the meantime, and once the operation *does* finish, it will invoke a **callback** that does any work that depended on the operation being complete.

In CoffeeScript, asynchronous code looks something like this:

```
bakePie ->
  slicePie()
whipCream()
```

What's going on here? `bakePie` is an asynchronous operation, and by convention it takes a callback as an argument. It will invoke this callback when it has finished, but that could be a long time from now! Because we can only slice the pie after it has finished baking, we put `slicePie` in the callback, so it will only be invoked when `bakePie` is finished. `whipCream` doesn't depend on the pie being in a certain state, so we simply call it immediately afterwards. Most of the time, `whipCream` will be called before `slicePie`!

Functions are the cornerstone of asynchronous programming in JavaScript and CoffeeScript. They allow us to defer operations until later, because the body of a function isn't run until that function is invoked. This lets us combine asynchronous operations with synchronous operations without adding a specific language feature to do it.

CoffeeScript's concise function definitions really shine when doing asynchronous programming. Just look at what the previous example looks like in JavaScript:

```
bakePie(function() {
  return slicePie();
});
whipCream();
```

I think you'll agree that the CoffeeScript version makes much more pleasant reading.

If you work with Node.js, you'll already be very familiar with asynchronous operations. Many operations that are synchronous in other server-side platforms are asynchronous in Node.js, and indeed this is why Node.js boasts very impressive performance in many situations.

If you work with client-side JavaScript, the most common place you'll encounter asynchronous operations is requests to remote resources. This makes sense—an HTTP request may take hundreds of milliseconds, eons in computer time. So we often do not wish to hold up all of our JavaScript code while we wait for a remote server somewhere to send us back a response.

Getting to know our remote API

Now that we know why asynchronous operations are important, let's go find one! We've decided to embellish the pet descriptions we display in our application when a pet is chosen from the list. In addition to information about the specific pet, we'd like to show some information about that breed. This will help our customers gain a better understanding of the animal they are interested in, and maybe teach them something extra!

Since we don't want to manage this extra information ourselves, we'd like to fetch it from another source, one who's in the business of compiling information. We're going to use a search engine, named DuckDuckGo, that's fast, powerful, and friendly to developers. DuckDuckGo provides an API to access their **instant answers** functionality. This is a feature that gives a concise summary for a search term, culled from various web sources they index.

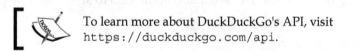 To learn more about DuckDuckGo's API, visit `https://duckduckgo.com/api`.

A typical query to this API is a simple GET request to a URL such as `https://api.duckduckgo.com/?q=miniature+horse&format=json &t=CoffeeScriptBook&pretty=1`. The `q` parameter is the search term for which we wish to get an answer. The `format` parameter specifies the format in which we'd like our response. We'll be using **JavaScript Object Notation (JSON)** because it is very easy to work with in JavaScript. JSON objects are valid JavaScript objects, so no parsing is needed to work with the data. The `t` parameter lets DuckDuckGo know whose application is making this request. The `pretty` parameter simply asks for the returned JSON to be indented for human eyes; we won't be using that parameter in our code, but it's nice while we're exploring the API.

Let's take a look at how a typical response from this API is structured. You can visit the previous URL in a browser and you will see the JSON rendered as plain text. Or, if you prefer to work in the terminal, you can use a program such as `curl` to make the request:

```
curl -i \
  'https://api.duckduckgo.com/?q=miniature+horse&format=json&pretty=1'
```

Here's what a response looks like, in part:

```
{
  "Definition" : "",
  "DefinitionSource" : "",
  "Heading" : "Miniature horse",
  "Image" : "https://i.duckduckgo.com/i/51e64c0a.jpg",
  "RelatedTopics" : [ ... ],
  "Abstract" : "Miniature horses are found in many nations,
    particularly in Europe and the Americas.",
  "AbstractSource" : "Wikipedia",
  "AbstractURL" : "https://en.wikipedia.org/wiki/Miniature_horse"
}
```

The `Abstract` field will be particularly useful to us. We'll also use the `AbstractSource` field and `AbstractURL` to properly cite the source of our information.

Making an asynchronous request

Let's start building our new feature! We'll add some CSS to style our new page element:

```
#pet_information .more {
  color: gray;
}

#pet_information .more p {
  border: 1px solid #CCC;
  border-left: none;
  border-right: none;
  padding: 1em 0;
  margin-top: 2em;
}

#pet_information .more a {
  color: #194900;
}
```

We'll trigger a lookup from `PetListView` whenever a new pet is selected from the list:

```
selectPet: (petIndex, element) ->
  petView = @views[petIndex]
  @renderToElement "pet_information",
    petView.formattedDescription()
  petView.renderExtraContent()
```

We need to add a container element to the bottom of the content rendered by our PetView:

```
formattedDescription: ->
  "<h2>#{@pet.name}</h2>" +
    "<h3 class='breed'>#{@pet.breed} " +
    "(#{@pet.age ? "??"} years old)</h3>" +
    @imageTag(@pet.image) +
    "<p class='description'>#{@pet.description}</p>" +
    "<div id='additional_info' class='more'></div>"
```

Now we just need to write the code to perform the request itself. Since this is a cross-domain request, we're going to use JSONP to avoid tripping over the same-origin policy. Using JSONP involves defining a callback to handle the received data, then calling the remote endpoint as executable JavaScript.

> To learn more about JSONP, see `https://niryariv.wordpress.com/2009/05/05/jsonp-quickly`. There is also a newer alternative standard, called CORS, that is more powerful and will probably eventually supplant JSONP. To learn more about CORS, see `https://developer.mozilla.org/en-US/docs/HTTP/Access_control_CORS`.

Let's write the `renderExtraContent` method on `PetView`. First we'll define the callback. We need to attach it to `window` to make it global, so it can be called by the remote script:

```
renderExtraContent: ->
  window.renderExtraContentCallback = (response) =>
    if response.Abstract
      @renderToElement "additional_info",
        "<p>#{response.Abstract} (" +
        "<a href='#{response.AbstractURL}'>#{response.
AbstractSource}</a>" +
        ", powered by <a href='https://duckduckgo.com'>DuckDuckGo</a>"
+
        ")</p>"
```

Notice that we must define the callback using a fat arrow. Recall from the previous chapter that the fat arrow binds `this` within the callback to the value of `this` in which the method was defined. In this case, we need to hang on to the object's context so that we can call `@renderToElement` inside the callback. You will find yourself using fat arrows extensively when working with asynchronous operations.

Once we receive a response, if it has an `Abstract` property, we render an element with the abstract's text and a link to the source. Now we'll build the request to fetch the data:

```
renderExtraContent: ->
  window.renderExtraContentCallback = (response) =>
    #...
  query = @pet.breed.replace " ", "+"
  url = "https://api.duckduckgo.com/?q=#{query}&format=json&t=CoffeeS
criptBook"
  s = document.createElement "script"
  s.src = "#{url}&callback=renderExtraContentCallback"
  document.body.appendChild s
```

We make a URL for the request, then create a new `<script>` element and set the source to our remote URL. Once we append that element to the document, it will automatically make the request and fire off the callback once it's received.

That's all we need. Our feature should be working, so let's check it out. Visit our application and click on one of the pets. Not all of the breeds will receive a result, so you may need to try a couple animals before you find one that works. Here's what it looks like:

Flops

French Lop (4 years old)

Enjoys nothing more than a good roll in the grass and a nap in the sun.

French Lop is a popular breed of domestic rabbit that was first developed in France in the 19th century out of selective breeding between the English Lop and the Flemish Giant. (Wikipedia)

Hooray! We've integrated our first third-party API!

While this works, the code required is a little convoluted, and it would quickly become painful if we needed to make AJAX requests in more than one place. In the next section, we'll solve that problem by integrating our very first third-party library.

Using a third-party library

For the sake of simplicity, we have so far refrained from using any third-party libraries. Now, however, we're going to pull in a library to help us make remote web requests. In the process, we'll also experience just how easy it is to integrate our CoffeeScript with a third-party library written in JavaScript. **Reqwest** is a small, focused library built specifically to help with AJAX requests, so it's perfect for us.

 To learn more about Reqwest, visit the project page at `https://github.com/ded/Reqwest`.

First, download the library from `https://github.com/iangreenleaf/reqwest/raw/coffeescript_book/reqwest.js`. Put this file in our application's directory and name it `reqwest.js`. Now we'll include it at the beginning of the JavaScript files in `index.html`:

```
<script src="reqwest.js"></script>
<script src="person.js"></script>
<script src="animal.js"></script>
```

We're ready to use Reqwest in `animal.coffee`. A typical `reqwest` call (in JavaScript) looks like this:

```
reqwest({
    url: 'path/to/data'
  , type: 'jsonp'
  , success: function (response) {
      console.log(response.content)
    }
})
```

The `success` property defines a callback that will be invoked when a response is received (as long as the response was successful, not an error).

The Reqwest library is written in JavaScript, but since CoffeeScript compiles directly to JavaScript, we can call `reqwest` from our CoffeeScript code like any other function. No tricks are needed to get it to work; it will compile down to the ordinary JavaScript invocations that Reqwest expects.

Let's replace all the code in `renderExtraContent` with a simpler version that uses reqwest:

```coffeescript
renderExtraContent: ->
  reqwest
    url: "https://api.duckduckgo.com/"
    data: { q: @pet.breed, format: "json", t: "CoffeeScriptBook" }
    type: "jsonp"
    success: (response) =>
      if response.Abstract
        @renderToElement "additional_info",
          "<p>#{response.Abstract} (" +
          "<a href='#{response.AbstractURL}'>#{response.
AbstractSource}</a>" +
          ", powered by <a href='https://duckduckgo.com'>DuckDuckGo</a>"
+
          ")</p>"
```

That's it! Our new code is much more concise. All the complexity of global callbacks and script elements has been abstracted away. Instead, we do the rendering inside the `success` callback, which Reqwest will call at the appropriate time. The library provides some other nice features, such as allowing us to pass our query parameters as an object rather than constructing the query string ourselves.

Refactoring

Our code looks much better, but it can still use a little improvement, and now is a great time to do that. The biggest warning sign is that our view is in charge of manipulating data and performing an API request. The view should not have to worry about these things—they are the model's job.

We'll leave our `renderExtraContent` method in place, but remove some of the body:

```coffeescript
renderExtraContent: ->
  @pet.fetchBreedInfo =>
    if @pet.breedInfo?
      @renderToElement "additional_info",
        "<p>#{@pet.breedInfo.description} (" +
        "<a href='#{@pet.breedInfo.url}'>#{@pet.breedInfo.source}</a>" +
        ", powered by <a href='https://duckduckgo.com'>DuckDuckGo</a>"
+
        ")</p>"
```

Now, instead of performing the request here, we will call a new method on the pet object itself, `fetchBreedInfo`. This method takes a callback that will be invoked when it's finished. This is a common pattern when working with asynchronous operations. If we need to extract a piece of code that uses a callback, the method we extract it to will often accept a callback as well. You can see that this preserves the logical flow of the method, even though we've extracted the actual AJAX request.

Now we'll define our `fetchBreedInfo` method in animal.coffee:

```
fetchBreedInfo: (callback) ->
  reqwest
    url: "https://api.duckduckgo.com/"
    data: { q: @breed, format: "json", t: "CoffeeScriptBook" }
    type: "jsonp"
    success: (response) =>
      if response.Abstract
        @breedInfo =
          description: response.Abstract
          source: response.AbstractSource
          url: response.AbstractURL
      callback()
```

The call to `reqwest` looks much the same as before. In the `success` callback, however, we don't render anything. Instead, we set the data we want as properties on this object, and invoke the `callback` that was passed in. Recall that in our case, this callback is the rendering method we just defined in our view code. However, the pet object doesn't really care what happens in the callback. It is simply signaling that it has finished fetching the data, and the caller may do whatever it pleases with that information.

Wrangling multiple asynchronous calls

Now that we're comfortable dealing with asynchronous operations, we'll take a look at a common use case: performing multiple asynchronous operations. The beauty of this paradigm is that these operations happen concurrently *by default*. Most especially with requests to remote web resources, which can often have a latency in the hundreds of milliseconds, it's hugely important that we can send a second request into the world without waiting for the first one to return. This ability comes with a few caveats, though. We'll look at some common pitfalls and learn how to navigate them with CoffeeScript's help.

We'll add a new section to our additional info. Displaying the summary text for a given breed is good, but we'd also like to provide some links to related topics. This way, especially curious visitors can click through to learn more about the animals we sell. One of the fields in the response from DuckDuckGo that we have not used yet is `RelatedTopics`. It holds an array of topics that are related to the one we requested. For example, the related topics for the search **French Lop** include **Lop rabbits**, **Pet rabbits**, and **Rabbit breeds**.

We'd like to show these topics, but to find the best link title, we'll need to perform another request to DuckDuckGo for each topic. From *that* response, we can pull the `Heading` property to use in our link.

Requests in a loop

First we need to come up with a list of topics. In `fetchBreedInfo`, we'll pull URLs out of the `RelatedTopics` field and pass them to another method:

```
fetchBreedInfo: (callback) ->
  # … =>
    callback()
    topics = (topic.FirstURL for topic in response.RelatedTopics when
      topic.FirstURL?)
    @fetchExtraLinks topics, callback
```

Now let's define `fetchExtraLinks`. It takes an array of topic links, and as before, a `callback` to call upon completion. For each of these topics, we'll need to perform an HTTP request to DuckDuckGo. We'll put the results into an object that the view can render on the page.

The good news is that since AJAX requests happen asynchronously, all of these requests can happen concurrently. This can make a big difference in responsiveness, since we'll only need to wait for two round trips (one round trip to fetch the initial list, and another round trip to fetch information for all the list items). If we performed these requests one at a time, we'd need to wait for potentially many round trips: 1 + the number of topics.

The bad news is that the asynchronous requests are going to introduce us to a very common mistake in JavaScript. Our first attempt at defining `fetchExtraLinks` might look like this:

```
# This code is incorrect!
fetchExtraLinks: (topics, callback) ->
  @extraLinks = {}
  for topic in topics
```

```
reqwest
  url: topic
  data: { format: "json" }
  type: "jsonp"
  success: (response) =>
    if response.Heading
      @extraLinks[response.Heading] = topic
      callback()
```

This *seems* like it should work great. We loop through the topics, calling our reqwest library for each URL. When we get a response, we add an entry to the @extraLinks property of the pet object with the topic heading as a key. Unfortunately, if we try this code, we'll discover that @extraLinks only contains one entry; the key is the last heading in the list, and the value is the URL of whichever request took longest to finish.

What happened? In JavaScript loops, the variable is a **reference** rather than a **value**, and it is reassigned on every step of the loop. Even though it looks like our callback has properly closed over topic, the value of topic changes before the callback has a chance to be invoked. By the time the HTTP requests finish, the loop has run all the way through and every callback sees a value of the final URL in the list.

This problem rears its head any time code inside a loop is not executed immediately:

```
# This snippet does not work as expected!
buggySleepSort = (numbers) ->
  for n in numbers
    setTimeout(
      -> console.log n
      n
    )
sleepSort [4, 2, 6, 9, 3]
```

We expect this to output **2 3 4 6 9**, but instead it outputs **3 3 3 3 3** (notice that 3 is the last number in the array, thus the last value assigned to n).

This function is an implementation of **SleepSort**, an extremely silly sorting algorithm that sorts a list of numbers by sleeping an amount of time proportional to the value of the list member. Since large numbers sleep for a longer amount of time, they will be printed later. For more information on SleepSort, see http://rosettacode. org/wiki/Sorting_algorithms/Sleep_sort.

This is simply a quirk in the JavaScript specification that we must live with. CoffeeScript cannot completely prevent it from happening, but it gives us an easy way to deal with the problem. Remember the do keyword that we used earlier to immediately invoke a function? It comes in very handy now. You can define arguments in the function invoked by do, and the function will be called with the variables of the same name in the calling scope.

```coffeescript
sleepSort = (numbers) ->
  for n in numbers
    do (n) ->
      setTimeout(
        -> console.log n
        n
      )
```

We can see what's happening by looking at the compiled JavaScript:

```javascript
_results = [];
for (_i = 0, _len = numbers.length; _i < _len; _i++) {
  n = numbers[_i];
  _results.push((function(n) {
    return setTimeout(function() {
      return console.log(n);
    }, n);
  })(n));
}
```

Now that it's wrapped in a function, when we reference n in our callback, we're no longer referencing the n defined by the loop. We're referencing an argument *with the same name* that was defined on this wrapper function, and called with the **value** (not the **reference**) of the outer n. This inner n is a regular argument that retains its value as expected.

Let's use the do trick on our pet method:

```coffeescript
fetchExtraLinks: (topics, callback) ->
  @extraLinks = {}
  for topic in topics
    do (topic) =>
      reqwest
        url: topic
        data: { format: "json" }
        type: "jsonp"
        success: (response) =>
          if response.Heading
            @extraLinks[response.Heading] = topic
            callback()
```

Much better! All the categories now show up as expected.

Flops

French Lop (4 years old)

Enjoys nothing more than a good roll in the grass and a nap in the sun.

French Lop is a popular breed of domestic rabbit that was first developed in France in the 19th century out of selective breeding between the English Lop and the Flemish Giant. (Wikipedia)

Learn more:

- Lop rabbits
- Pet rabbits
- Rabbit breeds

Determining when we're finished

Let's fix one more thing with our list of related links. Right now we're calling the callback after each additional link is received. This isn't totally sensible behavior. It's hard to claim that we're *done* when we've received only one of possibly several pieces of data. This insensibility bleeds through into the callback body, and the rendering we perform there. Links may pop onto the screen one at a time in random order. And if we are running on a platform with limited computational power, such as mobile devices, we very much want to minimize the number of times we force the page to be re-rendered.

We want to call the callback only once all the requests are finished, but this isn't totally straightforward in an asynchronous model. We can't just place it *after* our `for` loop like we would in synchronous code. Instead, we will keep track of how many requests are pending, and call the callback once they have all completed.

```
fetchExtraLinks: (topics, callback) ->
  @extraLinks = {}
  expected = topics.length
  for topic in topics
    do (topic) =>
      reqwest
        url: topic
        data: { format: "json" }
        type: "jsonp"
```

```
success: (response) =>
  if response.Heading
    @extraLinks[response.Heading] = topic
    expected -= 1
    callback() if expected is 0
```

We determine how many requests will be fired by checking the length of the list of topics. Then, with each completed request we decrement our counter and check if it has reached 0. This way, only the last request to finish (no matter which request it is) will call the callback.

Check the application to make sure everything is working. We should still be displaying the links, but now we are doing so in a more orderly and efficient manner!

Alternatives for managing asynchronous calls

We've now seen the general pattern for performing multiple asynchronous operations at once. While it wasn't *too* difficult to keeping track of the pending requests by hand, it can become tiresome if you have to do this often. It can also become more complex if you do not have as simple a starting point as the length of an array; for example, if you only perform a request when certain conditions are met, or if you perform more than one request per item.

There are a number of solutions available to help you manage asynchronous control flow. We'll look at a few of these and try applying them to our application. These are completely optional! There's nothing wrong with the code we just wrote, and in subsequent chapters we will continue to use that version. But it's a good idea to know what your options are, especially if you end up working on an application with a large number of complex asynchronous operations.

Promises

The first solution we'll explore is **Promises**. Promises are a popular pattern implemented in a number of libraries on both client-side and server-side. Instead of using callbacks extensively, Promise-based code has a synchronous appearance. Function calls return a result right away, but instead of the requested value, the result is a *promise* to return the requested value at some point in the future.

For a more detailed introduction to Promises, see
http://blog.parse.com/2013/01/29/whats-
so-great-about-javascript-promises/.

The key to accessing the final value of a Promise object is its `then` method. This method takes two arguments (both optional), a success callback and a failure callback. Calls to `then` may also be chained, to allow easy manipulation of the final value. Some Promise libraries also offer more options for combining and creating Promises, to make the pattern even more powerful.

Using Promises in our application

Any function may return a Promise object, so many different libraries implement Promises and can interoperate by obeying the same spec. Luckily, our Reqwest library offers Promises as an optional feature, so we can easily start using them for our HTTP requests. Let's try out Promises on a simple example first. We'll rewrite our `fetchBreedInfo` method, which is responsible for a single API query to find the explanatory paragraph:

```
fetchBreedInfo: (callback) ->
  reqwest(
    url: "https://api.duckduckgo.com/"
    data: { q: @breed, format: "json", t: "CoffeeScriptBook" }
    type: "jsonp"
  ).then (response) =>
    if response.Abstract
      @breedInfo =
        description: response.Abstract
        source: response.AbstractSource
        url: response.AbstractURL
    callback()
    topics = (topic.FirstURL for topic in response.RelatedTopics when
      topic.FirstURL?)
    @fetchExtraLinks topics, callback
```

We call `reqwest` as before, but do not specify a `success` callback. This signals Reqwest to return a Promise instead. To retrieve the result of our query, we call `then` on the returned Promise with a function to be invoked when the Promise is successfully fulfilled. This callback does all the same processing that existed before.

We can even remove the parentheses around our function call to cut down on visual clutter:

```
fetchBreedInfo: (callback) ->
  reqwest
    url: "https://api.duckduckgo.com/"
    data: { q: @breed, format: "json", t: "CoffeeScriptBook" }
    type: "jsonp"
  .then (response) =>
    # ...
```

The indentation on `.then` is enough for CoffeeScript to know the right thing to do.

Now that we've tried out Promises on a simple single HTTP request, let's move on to the more complicated case of `fetchExtraLinks`, which performs multiple concurrent requests. This will showcase one of the powerful ways to use Promises.

Given our list of topic URLs, we'll loop through them as before, but this time we'll use Promises instead of providing a success callback:

```
queries = for topic in topics
  do (topic) =>
    reqwest
      url: topic
      data: { format: "json" }
      type: "jsonp"
    .then (response) ->
      [response.Heading, topic]
```

Our calls to `reqwest` return Promise objects because we didn't provide a callback. We need to manipulate the data returned by each Promise, so we call `then` on the object and return a duple of the heading and URL. Thus the contents of the `queries` array is some number of Promise objects that will eventually return these duples.

We've got an array of Promises, but we still need to turn that into something useful. For this we're going to use another third-party library called **RSVP**. This is a small library for working with Promises.

 For documentation and more information on RSVP, see the project page at `https://github.com/tildeio/rsvp.js`.

Download the library code from `https://github.com/tildeio/rsvp.js/` `raw/2.0.0/browser/rsvp.js` and place it in our project directory. Now we can add it at the top of the JavaScript files required in `index.html`:

```
<script src="rsvp.js"></script>
<script src="reqwest.js"></script>
<script src="person.js"></script>
```

The RSVP method we're interested in is named `RSVP.all`. This method accepts an array of Promises and returns a single Promise that is resolved when all the Promises in the array are resolved. This is exactly what we want! Once all of our HTTP requests finish, this Promise will resolve and call the function we provide it.

```
fetchExtraLinks: (topics, callback) ->
  @extraLinks = {}
  queries = for topic in topics
    do (topic) =>
      reqwest
        url: topic
        data: { format: "json" }
        type: "jsonp"
      .then (response) ->
        [response.Heading, topic]
  RSVP.all(queries).then (links) =>
    for [heading, url] in links
      if heading
        @extraLinks[heading] = url
    callback()
```

`RSVP.all` takes the `queries` array as an argument. To use the result of this promise, we define a function that takes a `links` array. This array will contain all the values returned by the Promises in `queries`. In other words, it will be an array of our heading/URL duples! All that's left to do is iterate through those values and assign them to the `@extraLinks` object, then invoke the callback.

That's it! We were able to remove all the code using Promises, and a helper from RSVP let us simplify our code a bit and get the exact behavior we wanted. If we wanted to take this idea further, we could even modify the method signatures of `fetchBreedInfo` and `fetchExtraLinks` so that they returned Promise objects instead of accepting callbacks. I'll leave that to you as an exercise.

We can use Promises with other libraries as well. jQuery offers optional Promise support on its asynchronous calls, and has additional functionality such as `$.when()`, which serves a similar purpose to `RSVP.all`. We can even use Promises with regular JavaScript if we have the poor luck of working on a non-CoffeeScript project.

An async helper library

Next we'll look at a library called, simply, **Async.js**. This library does not introduce a new pattern for asynchronous code. Instead, it works with the standard callback structure, and provides utilities to make working with asynchronous calls easier and more powerful.

> For documentation and more information on Async.js, see the project page at `https://github.com/caolan/async`.

Download the library from `https://github.com/caolan/async/raw/v0.2.5/lib/async.js` and place the file in our project directory. Now we can add it at the top of the JavaScript files required in `index.html`:

```
<script src="async.js"></script>
<script src="reqwest.js"></script>
<script src="person.js"></script>
```

Using Async.js in our application

Since Async.js works within the standard asynchronous callback pattern, we don't have any updates to make to `fetchBreedInfo`. However, the library can help us tame the multiple concurrent operations happening in `fetchExtraLinks`. We'll start our refactoring by pulling the request code into a separate anonymous function defined within the method:

```
getExtraLink = (topic, done) =>
  reqwest
    url: topic
    data: { format: "json" }
    type: "jsonp"
    success: (response) =>
      if response.Heading
        @extraLinks[response.Heading] = topic
      done()
```

This function makes a single request for a single topic, and adds the result to the `@extraLinks` object when finished. The `done` argument is a callback to be invoked when this operation is finished.

Now that we've set up this function, it's extremely easy to invoke it for each topic in the list, with a little help from Async.js. We'll use one of the utilities, `async.each`, which invokes a function for each member of an array in parallel.

```
fetchExtraLinks: (topics, callback) ->
  @extraLinks = {}
  getExtraLink = (topic, done) =>
    reqwest
      url: topic
      data: { format: "json" }
      type: "jsonp"
      success: (response) =>
        if response.Heading
          @extraLinks[response.Heading] = topic
        done()
  async.each topics, getExtraLink, callback
```

For each link in topics, async.each will call getExtraLink, passing in the topic and the done callback (this callback is how async.each knows when each operation is finished). When all the operations have finished, async.each will invoke its third argument, our callback that indicates fetchExtraLinks has finished.

Once again, we were able to remove all the extra code to track the number of operations manually, instead delegating that work to async.each. Since Async.js works with a standard callback structure, it has integrated very naturally with the structure of our existing code.

While we've only explored one of the utility methods here, Async.js offers many more to easily handle a number of different asynchronous situations. It's a powerful and extensive library, yet easy to understand and use. Here are two more possible ways we could have structured fetchExtraLinks using other Async.js utilities.

We could use async.map, which maps the result of each operation to a result array:

```
fetchExtraLinks: (topics, callback) ->
  @extraLinks = {}
  getExtraLink = (topic, done) ->
    reqwest
      url: topic
      data: { format: "json" }
      type: "jsonp"
      success: (response) ->
        done null, [response.Heading, topic]
  async.map topics, getExtraLink, (err, links) =>
    for [heading, url] in links
      if heading
        @extraLinks[heading] = url
    callback()
```

Or we could use async.parallel, which simply takes an array of functions and runs them all in parallel, invoking a callback when finished:

```
fetchExtraLinks: (topics, callback) ->
  @extraLinks = {}
  operations = []
  for topic in topics
    do (topic) =>
      operations.push (done) =>
        reqwest
          url: topic
          data: { format: "json" }
          type: "jsonp"
          success: (response) =>
            if response.Heading
              @extraLinks[response.Heading] = topic
            done()
  async.parallel operations, callback
```

Async.js is usable with any application, since it needs no more built-in support than the standard callback-based asynchronous structure. It is also usable with pure JavaScript as well as CoffeeScript.

IcedCoffeeScript

IcedCoffeeScript is a variant of CoffeeScript that adds additional features for managing asynchronous code. Just like CoffeeScript, it uses a command-line compiler to transform IcedCoffeeScript code into JavaScript.

 For documentation and examples of IcedCoffeeScript, visit the project page at http://maxtaco.github.io/coffee-script.

We will install IcedCoffeeScript through npm, much like we installed CoffeeScript.

```
npm install iced-coffee-script
```

We will now have the `iced` command-line tool available to us. It takes the same options as the `coffee` tool, with one addition. After stopping our running `coffee` compiler, we'll invoke the `iced` compiler and set it to watch our project directory.

```
iced --runtime inline -c -w .
```

The `--runtime` option tells the compiler where to put some extra helper functions that IcedCoffeeScript needs. For client-side code, we should use either `inline` or `window`. The default option, `node`, is useful for server-side code in Node.js.

> IcedCoffeeScript files may have either a `.coffee` or `.iced` extension. In large projects, it may be useful to use `.iced` to explicitly declare the dependency on IcedCoffeeScript—the regular CoffeeScript compiler will *not* be able to parse `await`/`defer` constructs. For simplicity's sake, we'll leave everything as `.coffee`. As long as the `.coffee` files are passed to the `iced` compiler, it will interpret them as IcedCoffeeScript if necessary.

Using IcedCoffeeScript in our application

The key feature of IcedCoffeeScript is the `await`/`defer` construct. `await` signals the beginning of a block containing asynchronous code. The code following an `await` block will not be executed until everything within the block finishes. Within an `await` block, each `defer` indicates an asynchronous callback. If given arguments, `defer` will assign the arguments from the callback to variables, so that they may be used by later code. When all `defer` calls in an `await` block have finished, the block is finished and will continue on to the next line of code.

Let's see this in action by changing `fetchBreedInfo` to use IcedCoffeeScript syntax for its HTTP request:

```
fetchBreedInfo: (callback) ->
  await reqwest
    url: "https://api.duckduckgo.com/"
    data: { q: @breed, format: "json", t: "CoffeeScriptBook" }
    type: "jsonp"
    success: defer response
  if response.Abstract
    @breedInfo =
      description: response.Abstract
      source: response.AbstractSource
      url: response.AbstractURL
  callback()
  topics = (topic.FirstURL for topic in response.RelatedTopics when
    topic.FirstURL?)
  @fetchExtraLinks topics, callback
```

We use `await` before the call to `reqwest` to signal the beginning of an asynchronous call. The success callback is now `defer response`, which assigns the `response` variable to the result of the request (remember that in regular CoffeeScript style, the callback looked like `(response) =>`).

The amazing part is that following the `await` block, our code proceeds on as if it were a synchronous operation. We examine the contents of `response` and go about our business, but there is no callback in sight. This is all thanks to some very clever transformations IcedCoffeeScript does behind the scenes. Our code *appears* synchronous, but when executed, it will *run* asynchronous as always.

Curious about how IcedCoffeeScript pulls this off? Just like we did with CoffeeScript features we were curious about, feel free to examine the generated JavaScript for this function!

IcedCoffeeScript can also help us handle the more complicated case of multiple concurrent operations happening in `fetchExtraLinks`.

```
fetchExtraLinks: (topics, callback) ->
  @extraLinks = {}
  responses = []
  await
    for topic, i in topics
      responses[i] = [null, topic]
      do (topic) =>
        reqwest
          url: topic
          data: { format: "json" }
          type: "jsonp"
          success: defer responses[i][0]
  for [response, topic] in responses
    if response.Heading
      @extraLinks[response.Heading] = topic
  callback()
```

We are once again using an `await` block, but this time it encloses the entire `for` loop. By invoking `defer` for each member of the array, the await block will not continue until every request is finished. We've changed our code a little to fit with the IcedCoffeeScript style. We build a `responses` array that will hold duples of response data plus the topic URL. Using the index `i` from the `for` loop, we can assign the results of the HTTP request to the correct duple with `defer responses[i][0]`. Once the await block finishes, our responses array is fully populated and it's a simple matter of looping through it.

IcedCoffeeScript is perhaps the most magical of the solutions we have looked at. It sometimes requires you to structure your code in a certain way (as we discovered in our second example), but the reward is a powerful syntax that removes some of the spaghetti-esque nature of asynchronous operations, without removing your ability to reason about the flow of the code.

A word of caution about IcedCoffeeScript: be aware that it is a separate project from CoffeeScript. It is well-maintained and stable, but in the end there is no guarantee that it will precisely mirror the state of the CoffeeScript project. You may also find that some third-party libraries and tools will need to be tweaked to use the `iced` compiler instead of the `coffee` compiler. And of course, the IcedCoffeeScript syntax is one more thing that new contributors to your project may be unfamiliar with. IcedCoffeeScript may or may not be the right tool for your project; it's up to you to weigh the benefits against the possible downsides and decide what fits your priorities.

The three options we've covered are not the only tools available for managing asynchronous behavior, but they provide a good overview of the space. There is quite a bit of diversity to account for taste, existing tools, and the complexity of the asynchronous operations you wish to deal with. Hopefully you've enjoyed one or more of the options we covered. I find that delegating the work of asynchronous callback management helps me keep my code clean, concentrate on the more important behavior, and avoid silly bugs.

Summary

In this chapter, we:

- Learned how to make asynchronous AJAX requests with a callback to process the response.
- Integrated a third-party library for easier AJAX requests.
- Learned how to perform multiple asynchronous operations at once, and how to track when they finished.
- Used these skills to request information from DuckDuckGo's API and display it in our pet store application.
- Used Promises, Async.js, and IcedCoffeeScript to help us control the flow of asynchronous code.

Asynchronous operations are a common sight in JavaScript, and we got some useful experience working with them in CoffeeScript. We learned some helpful features of CoffeeScript that help us keep our operations on track, and we learned some good architectural principles to keep in mind when working with asynchronous code of any sort.

The features we've added in this chapter mark the end of the new functionality we'll be adding to our pet shop application. It looks pretty good, don't you think? We'll still be working with the application for the final chapters, but we'll be reorganizing and refactoring instead of adding new features.

Next chapter, we will deal with a subject that's sure to come up sooner or later: debugging. Our application has reached a sufficient level of complexity that we're likely to encounter a bug here and there. We'll be looking at some cutting-edge tools that help immensely when debugging the JavaScript generated by CoffeeScript.

9

Debugging

With any sufficiently large application, bugs are an inevitability. Our project has gone well so far, but sooner or later we are bound to run into some unexpected failures. In this chapter, we'll learn how to deal with errors using some powerful new tools that allow us to debug in a browser directly against our CoffeeScript source. We will:

- Add some data to our application
- Uncover a bug that we haven't noticed before now
- Debug the error using tools that let us work natively with CoffeeScript in the browser
- Fix the source of the error

If you haven't worked with a debugger before, there will be a lot of new concepts to cover in this chapter. It's okay, though—we'll work through a full debugging workflow that you can re-use, practice, and refine as you deal with bugs in your own work.

Discovering a problem

A new pet has arrived at the shop, so it's time to add him to the inventory. We'll add the following object to our `animalData` array in `animal.coffee`:

```
name: "Captain Chirp"
type: "bird"
age: 2
breed: "Parakeet"
description: "Nice enough, though he strikes people as a bit...
flighty."
```

But if we refresh the page, nothing shows up!

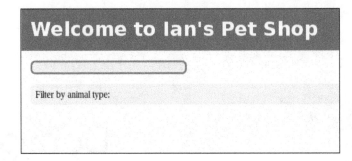

We've encountered an error in our code! Unfortunately, the error message is something like: **TypeError: behavior is null at pet_view.js:34**. This line number only applies to the compiled JavaScript, not to our CoffeeScript source.

One way to handle this is to find the corresponding line in `pet_view.js`, read the compiled code, and work backwards to determine which line in CoffeeScript generated the erroring JavaScript. Thankfully, CoffeeScript produces fairly readable output, and we've been learning throughout this book to understand how our CoffeeScript compiles to JavaScript, so this is often a viable method. Still, this becomes more difficult as code complexity grows, and even on simple problems it's a sub-optimal way to debug.

Luckily, a recent advancement in web technology has provided a better way to work with compiled CoffeeScript: source maps!

Working with source maps

Source maps are a great new idea from the web development community. They use a special map file format to trace characters of a served file (such as JavaScript or CSS) back to locations in a corresponding source file. This allows more transparency for automated file transformations such as compiling or minifying. If a file contains a special header or comment pointing to an accompanying `.map` file, the browser can read this source map to translate between the code it is running and the original source that it should display to the developer.

To read a full description of how source maps are implemented, see the proposed specification at `https://docs.google.com/document/d/1U1RGAehQwRypUTovF1KR1piOFze0b-_2gc6fAH0KY0k/edit`.

To work with source maps, we'll need to make sure that both our CoffeeScript compiler and our browser tools are up-to-date. Since this is a new technology, support for them has only been added recently.

We must use the CoffeeScript compiler from version 1.6.2 or later of CoffeeScript. It's easy to check what version you have installed:

```
coffee -v
```

If you don't have version 1.6.2 or higher, upgrade CoffeeScript using npm:

```
npm update coffee-script
```

Now we pass a special --map flag to the `coffee` command-line tool to tell it to use source maps:

```
coffee --map -w -c .
```

We can see that in addition to the `.coffee` and `.js` files, we also have `.map` files in our directory. This means our CoffeeScript compiler is successfully producing source maps.

Getting the right version of developer tools for our browser is a little more complicated, and depends on which browser we're using. We'll cover each browser separately below, so find and follow the section relevant to your browser of choice.

Source maps in the Firefox developer tools

Firefox has partial source map support in the **nightly** builds. These are packaged versions of the latest Firefox code under development (so named because a new package is compiled every night). These builds are not always as stable as official releases, but they are generally perfectly usable, and provide access to cutting-edge features that haven't been polished and added to the official stable releases yet.

> By the time you read this, source map support may have been packaged into an official release. These features are currently scheduled to be released with Firefox 24. If you have that version or higher installed, you can skip this step and try the following sections with your regular version of Firefox.

Visit http://nightly.mozilla.org/ and download the package for your operating system. Follow any necessary installation steps. Firefox Nightly is installed as an additional browser rather than replacing your existing Firefox, so you can run the two side by side.

Inspecting our application state

We're ready to get down to business. Open the developer tools by hitting
Ctrl + *Shift* + *K* (*Cmd* + *Opt* + *K* on a Mac), or choosing **Tools** | **Web Developer** |
Web Console from the menu.

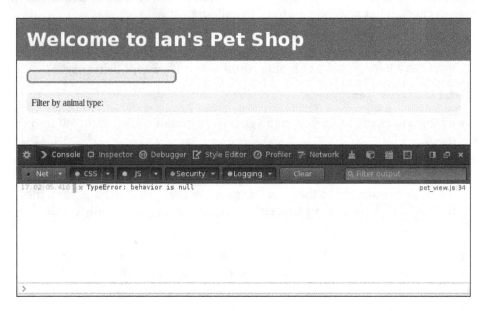

We can see our error, though right now the file and line number it gives us are for
the JavaScript file. We could look at that file and work our way backwards to the
CoffeeScript source, but there's an easier way to find the right line number.

> In future versions of Firefox, source map support will likely
> be expanded to show the CoffeeScript line numbers right in
> the console's error message. If this is the case in your browser,
> disregard the next step and simply click on the error trace to be
> taken to the CoffeeScript file.

Let's click over to the **Debugger** tab. At first, this will show us `.js` files. However, we
can turn on source map support by clicking on the cog icon in the upper right corner
to open the developer tools settings:

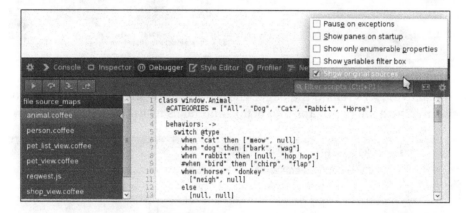

Enable the **Show original sources** option if it is not already turned on:

Once this is chosen, the file list will refresh and display our `.coffee` files instead. If we choose a file from the list, we'll see our CoffeeScript source right in the debugger!

Now we'll click on the cog icon again and enable **Pause on exceptions**. This will pause the page execution and bring us to the debugger when a JavaScript error occurs:

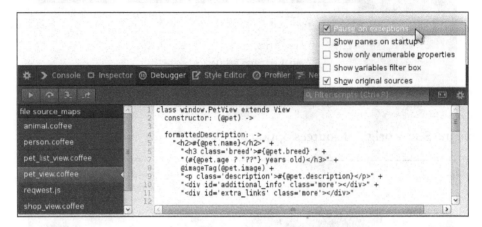

With this enabled, let's reload the page. The error we saw in the console will reoccur, and this time the debugger leaps into action and takes us to the source of the error!

There's a green marker in CoffeeScript code that highlights the line where the error occurred. The section to the right of this displays context information from the place the error occurred, such as the error itself, and any variables defined in that scope. The bar above the text area shows a stylized stack trace that we can click to see each level of the active function invocations, also in their original CoffeeScript locations.

Using the debugger

It's time to track down the source of our error. Starting with the line that raised the error, we can see that it's calling `behavior.toLowerCase()`. The right-hand panel shows us all the variables defined in this scope, and scrolling down to find `behavior` in this list confirms that it is indeed `null` right now. Calling `toLowerCase` on a null value is what caused our error.

We haven't solved our mystery yet. We know that the error occurred because `behavior` is `null`, but *why* is it null? We can see that `behavior` is being assigned, ultimately, to the results of `@pet.behaviors()`. We can also see, from the right bar, that the error is occurring while rendering the new pet we added, `Captain Chirp`.

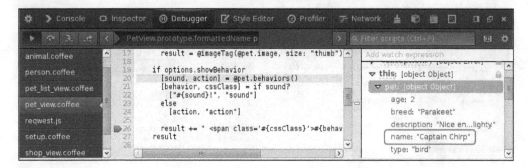

Armed with this knowledge, we're ready to dig a little deeper. We'll set a breakpoint on the call to `@pet.behaviors()` by clicking on the gutter next to it:

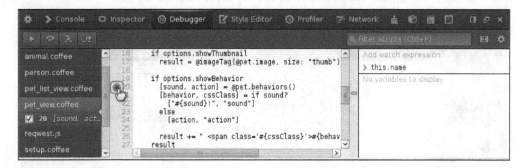

A blue dot will appear in the gutter to mark the location of our breakpoint. Now we can reload the page and the debugger will pause when it reaches that line of code:

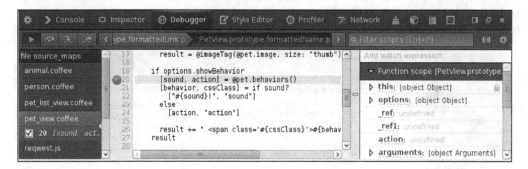

This code is invoked for each animal, but we're only interested in the invocation for `Captain Chirp`. We can easily keep track of which pet is currently under consideration by adding our own **watch expression** to the right-hand bar. Click on the text field, enter `this.pet.name`, and hit *Enter*.

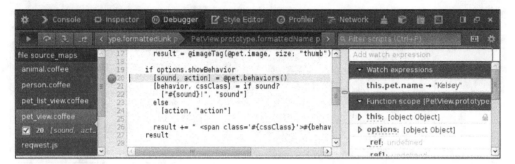

We'll now have a display of the pet's name that updates with the current environment. This way we can tell which pet the code is currently running against. To continue with code execution, hit the arrow button near the top left of the debugger:

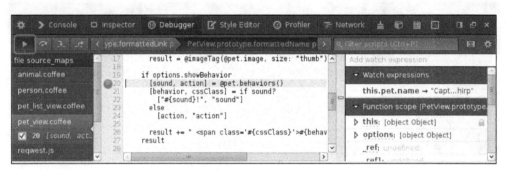

The script will continue running and pause again the next time we reach the breakpoint. Keep doing this until we reach `Captain Chirp`. Now, we'll hit the **Step In** button in the top left of the debugger. This takes us into the `pet.behaviors()` function definition:

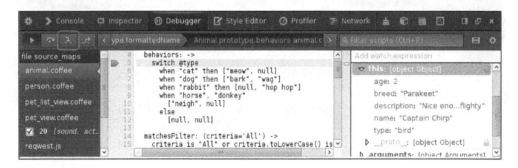

Now that we're here, we can reason out the cause of our problem. We see that the result of this function depends on the @type variable. By examining the values in the right-hand box, we can see that type for this pet is "bird". Looking back at the function definition, we realize that we have not defined a return value for a @type of "bird", so the switch statement will fall through to the default return value: [null, null]. Sure enough, we can hit the **Step Out** button to confirm this—it will take us to the result of this control structure:

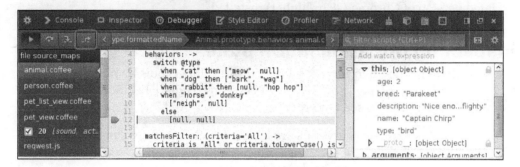

We'll hit **Step Out** once more to leave this function and return to the calling context. Here we can use the right-hand bar to confirm that sound and action are both null.

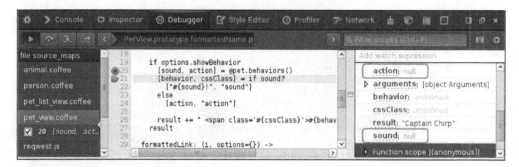

We can hit **Step Over** to run the if statement and pause on the next line, where the HTML output is constructed.

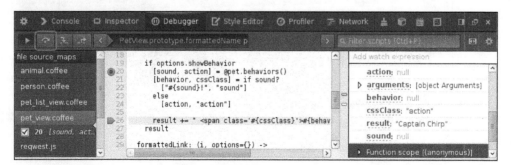

The right-hand bar confirms for us that `behavior` is `null`. We're back to the line we started on, but now we know why `behavior` is `null` and how we should fix it. Continue to the final section of this chapter to fix up our code and get rid of this bug.

Source maps in the Chrome developer tools

Recent versions of Chrome fully support source maps. Make sure you have a updated version of Chrome (28 or higher) installed.

Inspecting our application state

We're ready to get down to business. Open the developer tools by hitting *Ctrl + Shift + J (Cmd + Opt + J* on a Mac), or choosing **Tools | JavaScript console** from the menu, and we'll see our error.

If the file and line number it gives us are for the JavaScript file, we need to enable support for source maps (if it shows a CoffeeScript file, skip this step). Click on the cog icon at the bottom right of the developer console.

Now scroll down to the **Sources** section, and check the box next to **Enable source maps**:

Reload the page, and our console will now show a line number and file name for the CoffeeScript file!

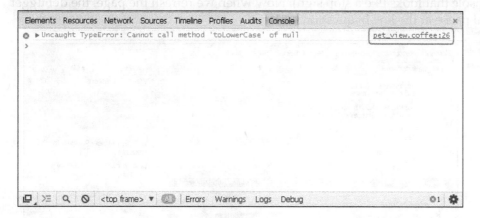

We can click on the filename and we will be taken to the **Sources** tab with `pet_view.coffee` open and the error and responsible line of code highlighted. This is our own CoffeeScript code, shown directly in the console and integrated with the error reporting and debugger!

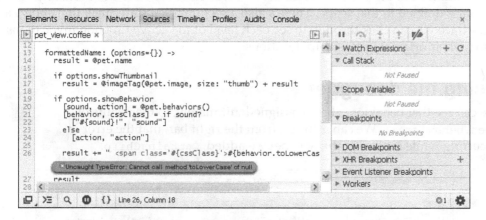

It's time to track down the source of our error. Starting with the line that raised the error, we can see that it's calling `behavior.toLowerCase()`. The error message informs us that `behavior` is `null`, and calling `toLowerCase` on a null value is what caused our error. We still have a mystery to solve, though. We know that the error occurred because `behavior` is `null`, but *why* is it `null`?

Let's use the debugger to pause the script execution at the point this error occurs. Enable the **Pause on all exceptions** toggle (it's a button along the bottom of the console that looks like a stop sign). Now when we refresh the page, the debugger will pause at the line in question.

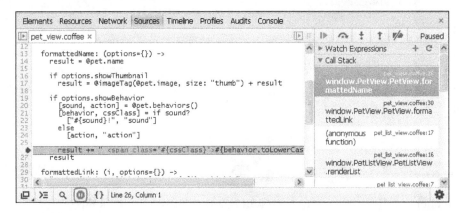

There's a red marker in CoffeeScript code that highlights the line where the error occurred. The section titled **Scope Variables** to the right of this displays context information from the place the error occurred, such as the error itself and any variables defined in that scope. There's also a section titled **Call Stack** that shows a stack trace we can click through to see each level of the active function invocations, also in their original CoffeeScript locations.

Using the debugger

We can see that behavior is being assigned, ultimately, to the results of `@pet.behaviors()`. We can also see, from the right bar, that the error is occurring while rendering the new pet we added, `Captain Chirp`.

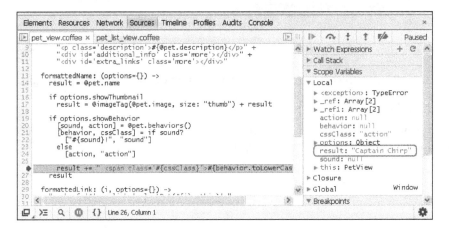

Armed with this knowledge, we're ready to dig a little deeper. We'll set a breakpoint on the call to `@pet.behaviors()` by clicking on the gutter next to it:

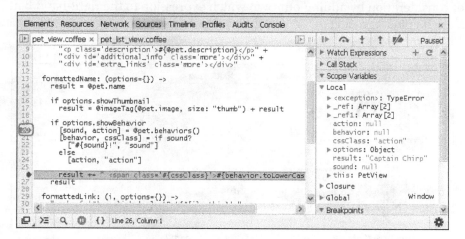

A blue marker will appear in the gutter to mark the location of our breakpoint. Now we can reload the page and the debugger will pause when it reaches that line of code.

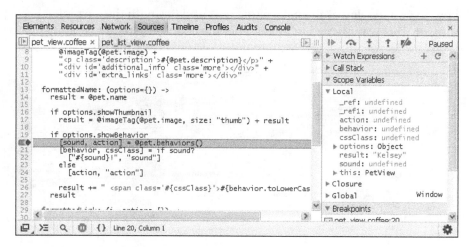

This line of code is invoked for each animal, but we're only interested in the invocation for `Captain Chirp`. We can easily keep track of which pet is currently under consideration by adding our own watch expression to the right-hand bar. Click on the plus sign next to the **Watch Expressions** section, type `this.pet.name`, and hit *Enter*.

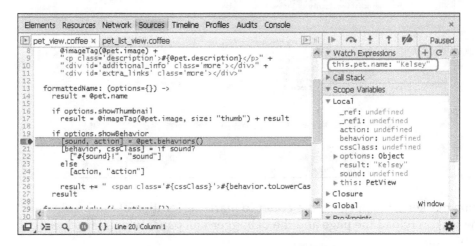

We'll now have a display of the pet's name that updates with the current environment. This way we can tell which pet the code is currently running against. To continue code execution, hit the play button at the top of the right-hand bar:

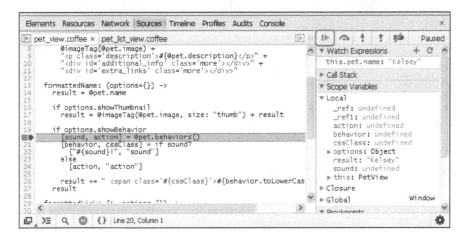

The script will continue running and pause again the next time we reach the breakpoint. Keep doing this until we reach `Captain Chirp`. Now, we'll hit the **Step In** button in that same toolbar. This takes us into the `pet.behaviors()` function definition.

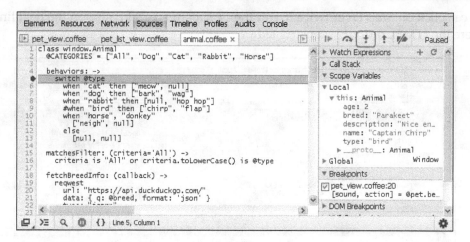

Now that we're here, we can reason out the cause of our problem. We see that the result of this function depends on the `@type` variable. By examining the values in the right-hand box, we can see that `type` for this pet is `"bird"`. Looking back at the function definition, we realize that we have not defined a return value for a `@type` of `"bird"`, so the switch statement will fall through to the default return value: `[null, null]`.

We can hit the **Step Out** button to leave this function and return to the calling context. Here we can use the right-hand bar to confirm that `sound` and `action` are both `null`:

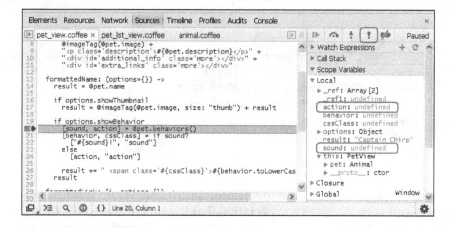

We can click on **Step Over** twice to run the `if` statement and pause on the next line, where the HTML output is constructed.

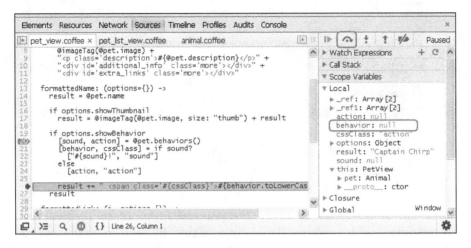

The right-hand bar confirms for us that `behavior` is `null`. We're back to the line we started on, but now we know why `behavior` is `null` and how we should fix it.

Fixing the problem

Let's open up `animal.coffee` in our text editor. First, we should add logic for birds if we're going to have them in our pet shop:

```coffee
behaviors: ->
  switch @type
    when "cat" then ["meow", null]
    when "dog" then ["bark", "wag"]
    when "rabbit" then [null, "hop hop"]
    when "bird" then ["chirp", "flap"]
    when "horse", "donkey"
      ["neigh", null]
    else
      [null, null]
```

Second, this bug occurred because the default return value from this function didn't play well with the caller's expectation that it would always be a string. Let's revamp our code in `pet_view.coffee` to properly handle the case in which all nulls are returned:

```coffee
if options.showBehavior
  [sound, action] = @pet.behaviors()
  [behavior, cssClass] = if sound?
```

```
    ["#{sound}!", "sound"]
else if action?
    [action, "action"]
else
    ["", ""]
```

This ensures that adding another unknown category in the future won't cause an error in our application. Instead, it will degrade gracefully and simply not display a behavior.

If we reload the page, our application is back to normal, and we know the bug has been successfully squashed!

Summary

Congratulations! We just debugged and solved a problem in CoffeeScript, without ever digging into the compiled JavaScript itself. We:

- Compiled our CoffeeScript with source maps
- Used the Firefox developer tools to debug CoffeeScript
- Used the Chrome developer tools to debug CoffeeScript

If you were not already familiar with debuggers, hopefully this experience has shown you how they can help you troubleshoot more efficiently and with less frustration. If you were already comfortable in a debugger, a lot of this probably felt familiar. Still, it's a wonderful improvement to be able to debug CoffeeScript code natively, right in the browser. Go forth and debug!

Now that we're comfortable with building and maintaining complex CoffeeScript applications, we're ready to start working on real-world systems. Often, this means integrating CoffeeScript into another framework. You may have an existing project that you'd like to use CoffeeScript in, or you may be looking to start a new project with a toolset that can handle the demands of organizing and packaging a project for deployment. Next chapter, we'll look at integrating CoffeeScript with some common web development frameworks.

10
Using CoffeeScript in More Places

I hope by now you're thoroughly excited about CoffeeScript! If so, you probably want to use it in *all* of your projects. Good news! This chapter is all about using CoffeeScript in more places.

It's possible to use CoffeeScript in just about any project, thanks to the handy `coffee` command-line tool. We can use that to compile our CoffeeScript into JavaScript, and then simply add the JavaScript files to our project. However, many common web frameworks can support CoffeeScript in a better-integrated fashion. We can often cut out the tedious middle step of compiling and moving around JavaScript, and instead write CoffeeScript and see the results immediately.

This chapter will cover integrating CoffeeScript into a number of common web settings. We will:

- Learn how to run CoffeeScript code directly in a browser
- Learn how to use CoffeeScript in our browser's developer console
- Learn how to build CoffeeScript in a Rails application
- Learn how to build CoffeeScript using Brunch, a web application assembler
- Learn how to build CoffeeScript in Node.js applications

CoffeeScript directly in the browser

Most of the time, we should compile CoffeeScript to JavaScript before serving it to a web browser. This provides much better performance and is guaranteed to work well across all browsers. However, it *is* possible to run CoffeeScript code directly in the browser! This magical feat is accomplished by sending a special version of the CoffeeScript compiler code to the browser, which may then be used to parse and compile CoffeeScript into JavaScript, and run it.

 This is thanks to the fact that the CoffeeScript compiler is itself written in CoffeeScript! So we can use the CoffeeScript compiler to compile *itself* into JavaScript! Is your mind blown yet?

We can add this ability right to our pet shop application. We need to download a standalone version of the CoffeeScript compiler. It's available from the CoffeeScript site: `http://coffeescript.org/extras/coffee-script.js`. We'll put this file in our main application directory. Now we'll include this library in our `index.html`:

```
<script src="coffee-script.js"></script>
```

Now we can add a script tag to `index.html` with some CoffeeScript!

```
<script type="text/coffeescript">
  alert "Welcome!"
</script>
```

Notice that our `<script>` tag has a `type` attribute of `text/coffeescript`. The compiler uses this to recognize code it should compile. If we load our page in a browser, we will see a nice welcome message!

It's even possible to include remote CoffeeScript files. The tag to do this looks like:

```
<script type="text/coffeescript" src="my_script.coffee"></script>
```

Unfortunately, the CoffeeScript compiler must fetch the file with an AJAX request, so we can't easily see this in action if we're running our pet shop application directly from a file. It will work in an application being served through a web server, though—any time the browser address is something like `http://localhost/`.

Using CoffeeScript directly in the browser isn't something you'll want to do a lot in production applications. But it can be very nice for quickly prototyping an idea, or in unusual situations where you don't have a server readily available to compile your CoffeeScript. For example, the official CoffeeScript site uses this compiler for its **Try CoffeeScript** interactive console.

CoffeeScript in the browser console

Another place you may wish to run CoffeeScript is in the console of your browser's developer tools. In *Chapter 1, Running a CoffeeScript Program,* we learned how to use the command-line CoffeeScript console to quickly try out new ideas. The browser console offers a similar opportunity, and it also provides access to the DOM. This is invaluable when working on frontend code, because we can interact with our existing page and call our existing functions. Browser consoles are available built in to browsers such as Firefox and Chrome, or available as a plugin such as Firebug.

The browser console is great, but it's an annoying context switch to go back to writing JavaScript in the console, and it prevents us from easily copying code that we want to keep back into our project. Wouldn't it be nicer if we could write CoffeeScript in the console?

A CoffeeScript console in Firefox

With Firefox, we can use Paul Rouget's **JSTerm** add-on. This tool adds a fully-featured console to the Firefox developer tools. This console can be set to a CoffeeScript mode that can execute CoffeeScript right in the browser environment.

We'll need Firefox 20 or higher to install this add-on. If you've been allowing Firefox to update automatically, you will have an acceptable version. If you want to check, open the **Help** menu and choose **About Firefox**. The window that appears will give a version number. As long as it begins with **20** or higher, you're good to go.

Since CoffeeScript support was only recently added to this add-on, we'll need to install the development version. First, download the `.xpi` file directly from `https://github.com/paulrouget/firefox-jsterm/blob/master/jsterm.xpi?raw=true`. Now, drag the file into a Firefox window to begin installation.

 If version 3.0 or higher of the JSTerm add-on has been officially published, you can skip the direct download and install it from the Mozilla site instead: `https://addons.mozilla.org/en-US/firefox/addon/javascript-terminal`.

A prompt will appear asking for confirmation. Click on **Install Now** to install the add-on.

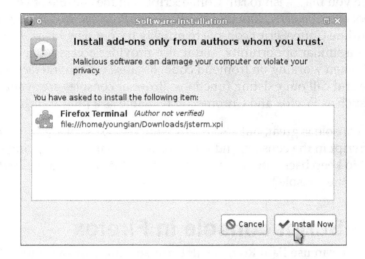

 You should not need to restart Firefox after installing this add-on. However, if you do not see a JSTerm console in the following steps, try restarting Firefox and the problem should go away.

Open the **Tools** menu, and check the box at **Web Developer | Toggle Tools**.

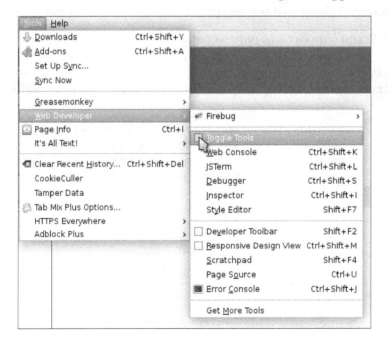

This will bring up the Firefox developer tools on the bottom of the window.

We should see a tab named **JSTerm**. Click on this and we'll be shown an interactive console. It expects JavaScript by default, so first we'll need to put it into CoffeeScript mode by entering the following command:

```
:coffee
```

Now we can run CoffeeScript and see it executed immediately. Let's try out the console by finding and modifying a DOM element. Navigate to our pet shop page and run the following code in the console:

```
header = document.querySelector "h1"
header.innerHTML = "Hello!"
```

We should see the top header content change from **Welcome to Ian's Pet Shop** to **Hello!**.

Great! Now we can use CoffeeScript right in the browser to play around with new ideas.

> The JSTerm add-on has many other useful features. You can learn
> more by entering the following command in the terminal:
> `:help`

A CoffeeScript console in Chrome

In Chrome, we'll use an extension by Jonathan Snook called **CoffeeConsole**.
This extension adds a tab to the Chrome developer tools that can run and
compile CoffeeScript.

Visit the Chrome Web Store to download the CoffeeConsole extension. You can
search for `CoffeeConsole` from anywhere in the store, or go directly to the extension's
page at `https://chrome.google.com/webstore/detail/coffeeconsole/`
`ladbkfdlnaibelfidknofapbbdlhadfp`. Click on **+ ADD TO CHROME**.

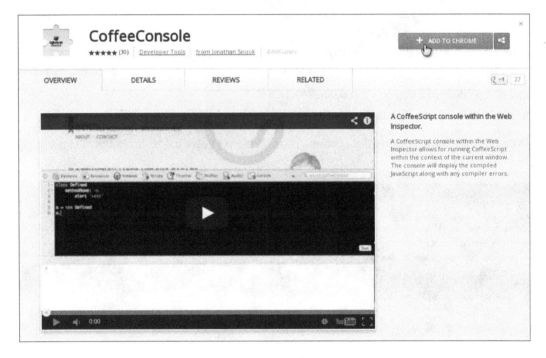

Click on **Add** at the prompt to install the extension.

Now open Chrome's menu, and navigate to **Tools | Developer Tools** (or simply hit *F12* to open them directly). This will bring up the Chrome developer toolbar on the bottom of the window.

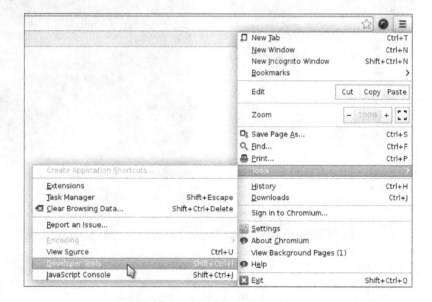

We should see a **CoffeeConsole** tab. Click on this and we'll see a split-pane window. Type `CoffeeScript` into the left pane, and we will see it instantly compiled to JavaScript in the right pane. Click on the **Run** button in the bottom-right corner to run our CoffeeScript in the browser environment.

Let's try out the console by finding and modifying a DOM element. Navigate to our pet shop page and run the following code in the console:

```
header = document.querySelector "h1"
header.innerHTML = "Hello!"
```

We should see the top header content change from **Welcome to Ian's Pet Shop** to **Hello!**.

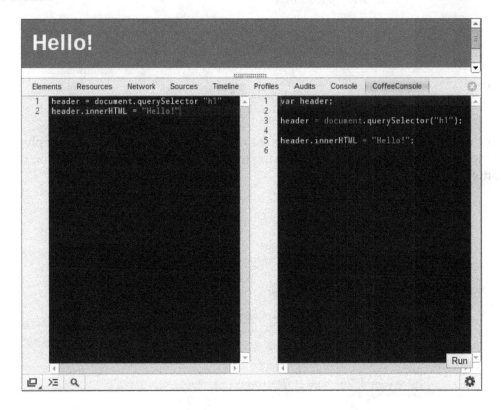

Great! Now we can use CoffeeScript right in the browser to play around with new ideas.

Using CoffeeScript with Rails

Ruby on Rails is a popular server-side framework for web applications. Rails has recently adopted first-class support for CoffeeScript, making it the preferred choice for client-side code in Rails applications. Rails uses an **asset pipeline** to compile CoffeeScript (among other things). This is some code that takes **assets** such as scripts and style sheets, and compiles and prepares them for consumption by a browser. We'll walk through the steps to get your CoffeeScript running smoothly in Rails with the asset pipeline, and we'll port our pet shop application to Rails to try it out.

Setting up the asset pipeline

The steps we'll need to follow depend on which version of Rails we are working with, and whether it is a new Rails application or an existing one. Please pick the appropriate section from the following for your Rails needs.

Creating a new Rails application

If you don't have an existing Rails application to work with, you should create a new one. This is very easy to do. You'll need to have Ruby installed – preferably version 1.9.3 or 2.0.x.

 Installing Ruby is beyond the scope of this book, but if you are having trouble, consider using **rvm** or **rbenv**. These tools can install Ruby to a non-system directory, and can manage switching between multiple versions of Ruby.

Install the Rails gem. To install Rails 3.2, use the following command:

```
gem install rails -v "~> 3.2.14"
```

Or to install Rails 4:

```
gem install rails -v ">= 4.0.0"
```

Now use the `rails` command-line tool to generate a new project.

```
rails new my_rails_project
cd my_rails_project
bundle install
```

For a new Rails 3 application, we'll want to remove `public/index.html`. It's a placeholder that we won't need.

Your Rails application is ready! Continue with the appropriate section below.

Rails 3.0

The asset pipeline is not officially supported on Rails 3.0. The best solution, if possible, is to upgrade to Rails 3.2. Having done that, follow the instructions for 3.1 and 3.2 to enable the asset pipeline.

If you are not able to upgrade Rails right away, it is possible to configure Sprockets to work with 3.0. Several example configurations are available online, such as this set of instructions: `https://gist.github.com/niuage/1112393`.

If you are unable to get Sprockets working with your Rails application, you can always fall back to compiling the files manually with CoffeeScript's command-line tool.

Rails 3.1 and 3.2

If you created your Rails application with Rails 3.1 or 3.2 from the beginning, or if you have already enabled the asset pipeline after an upgrade, you should be ready to go and can continue on to the *Setting up our application* section. However, if you have upgraded your Rails application from 3.0 or lower and have not enabled the asset pipeline, we'll need to make a few changes to enable it now. Add the following settings to `config/application.rb`:

```
require "sprockets/railtie"
module MyApplication
  class Application < Rails::Application
    # Enable the asset pipeline
    config.assets.enabled = true
    # Version of your assets, change this if you want to expire
      all your assets
    config.assets.version = '1.0'
  end
end
```

Add the following settings to `config/environments/development.rb`:

```
# Do not compress assets
config.assets.compress = false
# Expands the lines which load the assets
config.assets.debug = true
```

And add these settings to `config/environments/production.rb`:

```
# Compress JavaScripts and CSS
config.assets.compress = true
# Don't fallback to pipeline if a precompiled asset is missed
config.assets.compile = false
# Generate digests for assets URLs
config.assets.digest = true
# Precompile additional assets (application.js, application.css,
# and all non-JS/CSS are already added)
# config.assets.precompile += %w( search.js )
```

These changes configure the asset pipeline with sane behavior in all environments. In development, it will recompile assets on the fly so we can easily see our changes when we reload the page. In production, it will expect precompiled asset files that can be served without any performance overhead, and cached for a long time with the help of some cache-busting filenames.

We also need to add some gems to our `Gemfile` that the asset pipeline will use to do its work:

```
# Gems used only for assets and not required
# in production environments by default.
group :assets do
  gem 'sass-rails',   '~> 3.2.3'
  gem 'coffee-rails', '~> 3.2.1'
  gem 'uglifier', '>= 1.0.3'
end
```

 Since we have Node installed on our machine, Rails will detect that and use it as the JavaScript runtime for compiling CoffeeScript. However, if you wish to use the asset pipeline on a machine without Node, you may wish to use a gem called **therubyracer**. It's an alternative JavaScript runtime that may also be used to compile CoffeeScript and run other JavaScript on the server.

Be sure to install the new gems with this command:

`bundle install`

After that, restart the Rails server with this command:

`rails server`

Now we're ready to use the Rails asset pipeline! Continue on to the *Setting up our application* section.

Rails 4

Rails 4 has assets fully integrated by default, so there's not much we need to turn on. The only thing we should do is make sure that the CoffeeScript gem for Rails is in our `Gemfile`:

```
# Use CoffeeScript for .js.coffee assets and views
gem 'coffee-rails', '~> 4.0.0'
```

This is included by default, but make sure to enable it if it's not there.

We also want to disable Turbolinks in our project because we don't need it and it will interfere with our JavaScript. *Remove* the following line from `app/assets/javascripts/application.js`:

```
//= require turbolinks
```

Setting up our application

Now that our asset pipeline is set up and supports CoffeeScript, we're ready to add some. How will our CoffeeScript get included in the page? The primary JavaScript file for our application is found at `app/assets/javascripts/application.js`. We don't need to edit this file, but we should take note of the following line:

```
//= require_tree .
```

This is the **preprocessor directive** that tells it to require any other files in this directory. This way, when our page requests `/assets/application.js`, Rails will serve up all the scripts we've added, without us including each one manually. This script is included by the main layout automatically, so once we write a CoffeeScript file, it will show up.

We're going to create a simple controller and action so that we have a page on which to try out our CoffeeScript. If you already have actions defined in your Rails application, feel free to use those instead. Just make sure your layout is including the script we create.

Let's generate some scaffolding. Run the following command in our Rails project:

```
rails generate controller welcome index
```

We'll also set this as our root route so this page will act as our homepage. We can see that the `welcome/index` route has been added to our `config/routes.rb` by the generator. We'll add one more line below that to identify this as the root route.

For Rails 3.2:

```
get "welcome/index"
root :to => "welcome#index"
```

For Rails 4:

```
get "welcome/index"
root 'welcome#index'
```

Now we can run the development server with:

```
rails server
```

And we can see our new page at `http://localhost:3000/`. It will look like a generic placeholder page as shown in the following screenshot:

Welcome#index

Find me in app/views/welcome/index.html.erb

Adding some CoffeeScript

Now let's set up our pet shop application in Rails. First, we'll copy our `images` directory to `app/assets/images`. Let's copy `reqwest.js` into `vendor/assets/javascripts`. Copy and rename `style.css` to `app/assets/stylesheets/welcome.css.scss`. It's okay to overwrite the file that's there—it's just the placeholder for any styles related to this particular controller.

Next, we'll copy and rename `index.html` to `app/views/welcome/index.html.erb`, once again overwriting the existing file. We should edit this file a little. Rails uses a **layout** by default for all pages that takes care of the basic HTML structure, including tags for the CSS and JavaScript.

 You can find this layout file in `app/views/layouts/application.html.erb` if you need to edit it.

We can trim down our `index.html` to only the content within the `<body>` tag:

```
<h1>Welcome to <span id="owner_name"></span> Pet Shop</h1>
<div id="featured">
</div>
<div id="filtering">
  <span class="instructions">Filter by animal type:</span>
  <ul id="filtering_opts">
  </ul>
</div>
<ul id="available_pets">
</ul>
<div id="pet_information">
</div>
```

Now we just need to copy our `.coffee` files into `app/assets/javascripts`. There are a couple of changes we need to make to get our files working. First, we need to update our image paths. The Rails asset pipeline keeps everything under `/assets/`, whereas before we were keeping our images under `/images/`. Thankfully, we had the foresight to write a reusable helper for image tags, so we only need to modify one line of code, in `view.coffee`:

```
imageTag: (filename, options={}) ->
  options.size ?= "original"
  if filename?
    sizedFilename = filename.replace /\.(jpg|png)$/, "-
      #{options.size}.$1"
    "<img src='assets/#{sizedFilename}' />"
  else
    ""
```

The second change we need to make to our files is to set up dependencies between our scripts. We saw earlier that `application.js` will include everything in the `app/assets/javascripts` directory in the compiled JavaScript for this project. However, we need to help it determine a good order to pull the files in by specifying which files depend on which other files.

 As an added bonus, if we later want to include only some scripts on a given page, asset pipeline dependencies also make this very easy. We could simply require one file, such as `setup.coffee`, and every dependency will be pulled in automatically.

In the Rails asset pipeline, dependencies look like a special comment with a = and a `require` statement. These are read by the asset compiler when it's preparing to serve the files. No file extension is necessary — the compiler will determine it automatically.

We'll add a dependency on `view.coffee` in `pet_view.coffee`, since our `PetView` class extends `View`.

```
#= require view
class window.PetView extends View
```

We'll add this same line to `shop_view.coffee` and `pet_list_view.coffee`, since those classes also depend on `View`.

The third-party `reqwest` library is only used in `animal.coffee`, so we'll add a `require` directive there.

```
#= require reqwest
class window.Animal
```

And `pet_list_view.coffee` uses the `Animal` class, so we'll add a second `require` directive to that file.

```
#= require view
#= require animal
class window.PetListView extends View
```

We're almost done. Just one more script to change: `setup.coffee`. That file pulls in all the other classes, so it should have a number of `require` directives.

```
#= require person
#= require animal
#= require pet_view
#= require pet_list_view
#= require shop_view
shop = { … }
```

Since we're using Rails' layout, our JavaScript is now being included at the beginning of the page. We need to modify our initialization in `setup.coffee` to wait until the page is ready before trying to manipulate the DOM. Luckily, Rails comes with jQuery included by default, so it's very easy to put our code into a function that jQuery will run on ready:

```
$ ->
  petViews = (new PetView pet for pet in shop.animals)
  petListView = new PetListView petViews, shop.featured
  mainView = new ShopView shop.owner, petListView
  mainView.render()
```

With that, we should be ready. Reload the browser and we'll see our pet shop up and running, now backed by Rails!

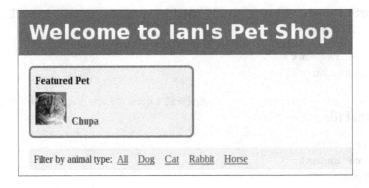

You'll notice the compiled JavaScript files don't exist anywhere in the project directories. In the development environment, Rails generates them automatically on demand. This means they are always compiled to reflect the most recent changes — no need to run the `coffeescript` command-line tool in the background. And we don't need to check compiled JavaScript files into our version control system. Instead, we will check in the source CoffeeScript files, and build the JavaScript as needed.

Precompiling assets

In the production environment, it's too slow to build our assets dynamically for each request. Instead, Rails provides a Rake task to **precompile** the asset files. Run the following command in the project directory:

```
RAILS_ENV=production rake assets:precompile
```

Now we'll find several `.js` files in `public/assets`. These are compiled and minified versions of our scripts, ready to be served directly from the server. If we look at `public/assets/application.js`, most of it is the minified jQuery library, but down near the very bottom we can see our code compiled in.

Since your development environment doesn't use these precompiled assets, you don't need to leave them lying around. Rails provides a rake task to remove compiled assets.

Rails 3:

```
rake assets:clean
```

Rails 4:

```
rake assets:clobber
```

If this is your first time using the asset pipeline in your app, you'll want to add a step to your deployment process to precompile the assets on the production server. If you're using **Capistrano** to do your deploys, it's as easy as adding the following line to `deploy.rb`:

```
load 'deploy/assets'
```

Using CoffeeScript with Brunch

If your application is completely client-side, you don't need a server framework like Rails or Node to execute backend logic, but you still need a way to build your assets. If CoffeeScript is the only preprocessing you need to do on your application, the simplest way to do this is using the command-line tool. However, you might want a more formal framework for organizing your project, or you might have other build steps involved in preparing your client-side project.

Brunch is a very popular choice for these situations. Brunch describes itself as an "assembler for HTML5 applications". It can compile a number of popular formats into their web-ready counterparts, like Haml into HTML, Sass into CSS, and of course CoffeeScript into JavaScript. Brunch also packages, concatenates, and minifies these files so you can write code without worrying about the build step. We'll port our pet shop application to Brunch to try out the CoffeeScript compilation and other features Brunch has to offer.

Creating a Brunch project

Let's create a simple Brunch application. First, we're going to install the `brunch` package globally using **npm**, the Node package manager we used to install CoffeeScript.

```
npm install -g brunch
```

 Make sure you have version 1.6.7 or greater of the `brunch` package installed. Otherwise you may not get the right template.

Now we can use the `brunch` command-line tool to start a new project. We're going to specify a special bare-bones template to base our project on.

If no template is given, Brunch will create a project that uses **Chaplin.js**, a client-side JavaScript framework. Chaplin is a very nice project in its own right, but outside the scope of this book. Visit `http://chaplinjs.org/` for more information.

```
brunch new --skeleton \
  github:monokrome/brunch-with-brunch my_brunch_project
cd my_brunch_project
```

We can see that this folder has been filled out with an application skeleton. Most of our application logic will go in `app`. Third-party libraries will go in `vendor`.

 For more information about Brunch and guides on how to configure and structure your Brunch application, see `http://brunch.io/#documentation`.

Let's fire up the application to see it in action. Brunch's command-line tool can also be used to build our source code into a ready-to-use application. It comes with a `watch` mode similar to the CoffeeScript tool that will recompile the project any time a file changes. As an added bonus, this mode can run a development web server to view out project. Start it up with the following command:

```
brunch watch --server
```

Now we can view our site by visiting `http://localhost:3333/`. Right now we'll only get an error message because we're missing `index.html`, but this is enough to see that Brunch is working.

```
Error: ENOENT, stat 'public/index.html'
```

Filling out our application

First we'll create the `app/assets` directory to hold all our static files. Now let's copy the contents of our application's `images` directory into `app/assets`. We'll also copy `index.html` into `app/assets`.

Next, we'll copy `reqwest.js` into `vendor` and copy `style.css` into `app`. Finally, we'll copy all our `.coffee` files into `app` as well.

We should add CoffeeScript support so that Brunch can compile our code. We'll use a special compatibility package built to wire CoffeeScript up to the Brunch pipeline. Add the following line to the dependencies list in `package.json`:

```
"dependencies": {
  "javascript-brunch": ">= 1.0 < 1.6",
  "coffee-script-brunch": ">= 1.0 < 1.7",
  "css-brunch": ">= 1.0 < 1.6",
  "uglify-js-brunch": ">= 1.0 < 1.6",
  "clean-css-brunch": ">= 1.0< 1.6"
}
```

Make sure to install the new dependency with npm:

npm install

We need to make a couple of changes to `index.html`. We'll change the CSS link to `app.css`, since that's the default used by Brunch:

```
<head>
  <title>The Pet Shop</title>
  <link href="/stylesheets/app.css" media="screen"
    rel="stylesheet" type="text/css" />
</head>
```

And we'll remove all our JavaScript include tags and replace them with two tags, an application script and a vendor script:

```
<script src="/javascripts/vendor.js"></script>
<script src="/javascripts/app.js"></script>
```

`vendor.js` holds any third-party scripts, such as our Reqwest library. `app.js` holds our own application's code. Brunch automatically concatenates everything into one file, which is much more convenient than keeping track of everything on our own.

> It's possible to fine-tune the way Brunch compiles our assets using the `config.coffee` file. See the Brunch documentation for more information at `https://github.com/brunch/brunch/blob/master/docs/config.md`.

Finally, right after our JavaScript includes, we need to add a single line of inline JavaScript to kick off our application:

```
<script src="/javascripts/vendor.js"></script>
<script src="/javascripts/app.js"></script>
<script>require("setup")</script>
```

Brunch uses a **CommonJS**-style system to separate pieces of JavaScript into **modules** — pieces of code with their own scope. This reduces conflicts and helps load things in the right order. The line we added simply loads the `setup` module to execute the code in `setup.coffee`.

As part of the module system, every script file is wrapped in an anonymous function before being included in the compiled JavaScript. This is very similar to what CoffeeScript does by default to protect the global scope. In CommonJS, the way to declare what part of a file should be exposed to the world is to assign it to `module.exports`. Whatever you assign is what will be available to other code that requires this module. Let's adjust `person.coffee` to meet this new requirement.

```
module.exports = class window.Person
```

Since we are explicitly pulling modules into scope, we no longer need to assign our classes to the global `window` object. Let's fix that:

```
module.exports = class Person
```

Nice! Now we can give `animal.coffee` the same treatment:

```
module.exports = class Animal
```

And `view.coffee`:

```
module.exports = class View
```

When one module wants to make use of another, it needs to bring it into scope using `require`. We'll require the `view` module from `pet_view.coffee`, since our `PetView` class extends `View`.

```
View = require "view"
module.exports = class PetView extends View
```

This makes sure that `View` is defined within the scope of the `pet_view` module. Notice that we've also added a `module.exports` assignment so this may be required elsewhere.

We give the same treatment to `shop_view.coffee`:

```
View = require "view"
module.exports = class ShopView extends View
```

And to `pet_list_view.coffee`, though this one also needs to pull in the `Animal` class:

```
View = require "view"
Animal = require "animal"
module.exports = class PetListView extends View
```

There's just one more thing to do. We need to pull in every class that is used in `setup.coffee`.

```
Person = require "person"
Animal = require "animal"
PetView = require "pet_view"
PetListView = require "pet_list_view"
ShopView = require "shop_view"
shop = { … }
```

That's it! Now our `index.html` will require the `setup` module, which will pull in everything else.

 What about scripts in `vendor`? Those aren't subjected to the CommonJS module wrapping by default, so they are still available in the global scope.

Our Brunch application is ready! If our server is still running, when we refresh the browser we should see our pet shop, ready to go!

Congratulations! We have a working Brunch application. There's plenty more to learn about these tools, but that's enough to get you started.

Precompiling assets

In the production environment, we won't want to run Brunch's built-in server. It's too slow to build our assets dynamically for each request, and we shouldn't need a separate process — we should be able to serve up our static files with whatever web server we're using. Brunch provides a `build` command to create these files:

```
brunch build
```

When that command finishes, we can find our files in the `public` directory. The compiled CoffeeScript will be in `public/javascripts/app.js`. If we're building for a production environment, we may also want to minify our JavaScript and CSS to reduce download times. Brunch will do this for us given an additional flag:

```
brunch build --optimize
```

The files will be in the same place as before, but now they are minified.

Using CoffeeScript with Node.js

Node.js is an environment that runs JavaScript on the server side. We're already using it to run our CoffeeScript compiler! However, Node is also popular for running server applications. It should be no surprise, then, that we can configure server-side Node applications to compile CoffeeScript for client-side code.

We'll build a simple server using Express, a popular MVC framework for Node. To compile our CoffeeScript, we'll use a Node package that provides an **asset pipeline**. This is some code that takes **assets**, such as scripts and style sheets, and compiles and prepares them for consumption by a browser. Once we have that set up, we'll port our pet shop application to try it out.

Even though we'll be detailing the process with Express, this system will work on many Node applications. Our asset pipeline package works as a **Connect middleware**. This is a common format for building interoperable plugins to web servers in Node. If your chosen server supports Connect middleware, it should be able to support CoffeeScript using a very similar process to that described here.

Creating our project

We already have npm installed, so we can use that to install the Express package globally.

```
npm install -g express
```

This gives us access to the `express` command-line tool, which we can use to generate a new Express project.

```
express --ejs my_node_project
cd my_node_project
npm install
```

We can run our new application in Node:

```
node app.js
```

Now we can visit our application at `http://localhost:3000/`. We should see a simple placeholder screen that Express provides.

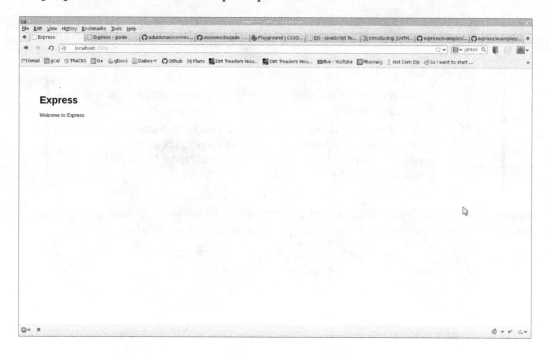

Keeping the server up-to-date

When we make changes to our files, we generally want our development server to load the latest file so we can see the results in our browser right away. Most Node servers don't do this automatically, but we can get this behavior by installing a simple helper tool that will watch the files and restart our server process when it sees changes. We'll install this tool globally:

```
npm install -g supervisor
```

Shut down the running server with *Ctrl+C* if you haven't yet. Now, instead of running the server with `node`, we'll run it with `supervisor`:

```
supervisor app.js
```

Since we will be editing CoffeeScript and EJS files, we want to make sure `supervisor` watches those file extensions for changes. We'll pass it a flag to include those extensions:

```
supervisor --extensions 'js|coffee|ejs' app.js
```

Let's try it out. Open up `routes/index.js` and change the `title` attribute to something else:

```
exports.index = function(req, res){
  res.render('index', { title: "Ian's Pet Shop" });
};
```

Hang on, why are we editing JavaScript? I thought this book was about CoffeeScript!

Well, we're going to use CoffeeScript for our client-side code, but right now our server-side code is in JavaScript. It's very much possible to run CoffeeScript on the server in Node, but we'll cover that later in *Chapter 11, CoffeeScript on the server*.

Supervisor should print a message in the console to let us know it detected changes, and if we reload our browser, our change will appear automatically!

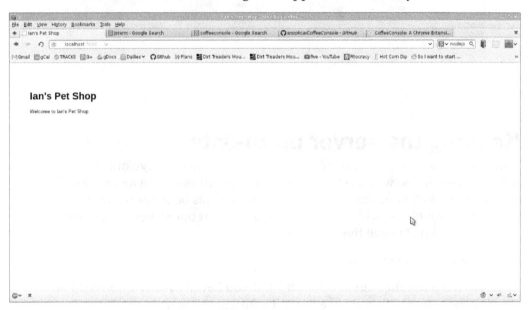

Now we're ready to edit our application and see the changes immediately, without needing to fiddle with the server terminal.

Adding CoffeeScript compilation

Create an `assets/js/` directory. Now copy all the `.coffee` files for our application into it, as well as `reqwest.js`. You don't need to copy all the generated `.js` files—those will be generated automatically.

We need to edit our package.json file. This file describes the project and specifies npm package dependencies that it needs to run. The express and ejs packages are already listed there. We're going to add connect-assets, our asset pipeline package, and coffee-script to do the compilation.

 Even though we've installed coffee-script globally and have been using that throughout this book, specifying it here will install it locally in this project directory. This keeps all the project dependencies in one place, and is very useful when different projects may need different versions of the same package.

```
"dependencies": {
  "express": "3.2.4",
  "connect-assets": "2.4.x",
  "coffee-script": "1.x",
  "ejs": "*"
}
```

Since we've changed the dependencies, let's use npm to install them:

npm install

Now that we have the assets package installed, we need to instruct our application to use it. We'll edit app.js to pull in the assets package:

```
var express = require('express')
  , assets = require('connect-assets')
  , routes = require('./routes')
  # ...
```

And further down that file, we'll call app.use, which is the mechanism Express uses to activate middleware packages.

```
# ...
app.use(app.router);
app.use(assets());
```

This should be enough to enable compilation of CoffeeScript files in our project! Now we just need to fill in the rest of the application so we have something to run our scripts.

Finishing our application

First we'll copy the contents of our application's images directory right into public/images. These will now be available through the Express server.

Let's copy the `index.html` file from our application into this new project. We'll rename it to `views/index.ejs`, overwriting the existing file by that name (it's just the placeholder Express created, and we no longer need it). The `.ejs` extension identifies this as an **EJS** template. EJS is a format for embedding small pieces of dynamic data in HTML files, but for the most part it still looks and behaves like HTML.

We'll need to make one change to `index.ejs`. Instead of writing the `<script>` tags ourselves, we'll use the `js` helper that's provided by `connect-assets`.

```
    . . .
    <%- js("reqwest") %>
    <%- js("person") %>
    <%- js("animal") %>
    <%- js("view") %>
    <%- js("pet_view") %>
    <%- js("pet_list_view") %>
    <%- js("shop_view") %>
    <%- js("setup") %>
  </body>
</html>
```

This helper will output script tags with the correct path, and it alerts the compiler to prepare those files. You may also notice that we don't need to provide file extensions. The asset compiler automatically finds the right file, whether it's `.js` or `.coffee`.

The `<%-` and `%>` tags are the syntax EJS uses to enclose dynamic parts of the template. Most of the time, EJS templates use `<%=`, but we need to output raw HTML instead of having it escaped, so we use the `<%-` variant instead.

We could throw our style sheet right into `public/stylesheets`, but since we've got the asset compiler all set up, let's go ahead and use that. This will keep everything in one place, make it easier to manage our style sheets, and allow us to use CSS precompilers in the future if we want to. Create an `assets/css` directory, and copy `style.css` into it. Now we'll edit `index.ejs` again to use the `css` helper to link to our style sheet.

```
<head>
  <title>The Pet Shop</title>
  <%- css("style") %>
</head>
```

`connect-assets` can also compile CSS files from the popular **Stylus** and **Less** preprocessor formats. These formats can make life much easier when dealing with large style sheets and complicated rules. For more information, see the `connect-assets` documentation at `https://github.com/adunkman/connect-assets`.

That's it! Our server running under `supervisor` should have automatically restarted to get the latest changes, so if we reload our browser we should see our pet shop application. It looks the same as before, but now it's powered by a slick Node.js backend and a powerful asset pipeline!

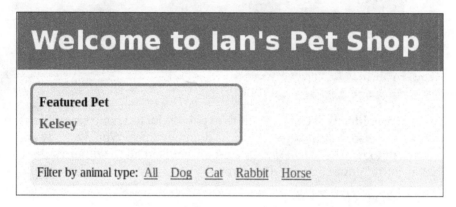

Cleaning up our script dependencies

There's an easy step we can take that will greatly improve our new Express application. Rather than managing all our script files by hand, we can specify which files depend on which other files. Then, the asset pipeline can use that information to know which files to use and what order to serve them in. It makes our lives easier and our application more efficient.

In `connect-assets`, dependencies look like a special comment with a = and a `require` statement. These are read by the asset compiler when it's preparing to serve the files. No file extension is necessary—the compiler will determine it automatically.

We'll add a dependency on `view.coffee` in `pet_view.coffee`, since our `PetView` class extends `View`.

```
#= require view
class window.PetView extends View
```

We'll add this same line to `shop_view.coffee` and `pet_list_view.coffee`, since those classes also depend on `View`. Now we can remove the explicit `js("view")` call from `index.ejs`. Instead, it will automatically be included when one of the files that depends on it is requested.

This is a good start, but there's more we can do, and it will pay off when we finish. The third-party `reqwest` library is only used in `animal.coffee`, so we'll add a `require` directive there.

```
#= require reqwest
class window.Animal
```

And `pet_list_view.coffee` uses the `Animal` class, so we'll add a second `require` directive to that file.

```
#= require view
#= require animal
class window.PetListView extends View
```

We're almost done. Ideally we only want to explicitly include one script file on our page—everything else should be pulled in as dependencies. Well, we only actually expect one script to run: `setup.coffee`. That file pulls in all the other classes, so it should have a number of `require` directives.

```
#= require person
#= require animal
#= require pet_view
#= require pet_list_view
#= require shop_view
shop = { … }
```

Now we can radically simplify the script includes in `index.ejs`:

```
    . . .
    <%- js("setup") %>
  </body>
</html>
```

Everything setup needs to run will be found and included in an appropriate order by `connect-assets`. And when it's building for a production environment, it will concatenate everything into one file to reduce the number of network requests. Using an asset pipeline has both made our code easier to manage, and more performant—a win-win!

Summary

In this chapter, we learned how to integrate CoffeeScript using:

- A special version of the CoffeeScript compiler that runs directly in the browser
- Browser add-ons to support CoffeeScript in the developer console.
- The Rails asset pipeline
- Brunch, the web application assembler
- A Node package that provides an asset pipeline as Connect middleware

This chapter was all about finding the tools to bring convenient, well-organized CoffeeScript support to our favorite web frameworks. Hopefully you've been able to use these on a project or two that was desperately in need of CoffeeScript's eloquent syntax.

There's one more place to use CoffeeScript that we haven't covered yet: the server! Next chapter, we'll learn all about using CoffeeScript in Node.js, and we'll try it out by porting the Express application we wrote in this chapter from JavaScript to CoffeeScript.

11

CoffeeScript on the Server

Until now, almost all our CoffeeScript code has been written to run in a browser. Our web application is a fully client-side system backed by static content. This has worked well for us so far, but it's time for bigger and better things. We're going to venture onto the server and learn how to run CoffeeScript code in **Node.js**. We'll take this opportunity to turn our web application into a dynamic system that can respond to user input.

We will:

- Convert our Node application to CoffeeScript
- Give our server some additional responsibility for handling data
- Use a simple database to make our application dynamic
- Encapsulate common development tasks with an easy command-running tool

Running a server with CoffeeScript

In *Chapter 10, Using CoffeeScript in More Places*, one of the systems we looked at was a Node server using Express. At that time, we left the server code in JavaScript and focused on using connect-assets to compile our client-side CoffeeScript into JavaScript. Now, we're going to use that Express application again, but we'll be working on the server-side code. And you guessed it—we'll be writing CoffeeScript.

 Our package.json already includes coffee-script as a dependency, since we're using it for asset compilation. If it didn't, though, we would need to add coffee-script to the devDependencies to make sure our development tools have access to the CoffeeScript compiler.

We'll start with the Express server JavaScript code from *Chapter 10, Using CoffeeScript in More Places*. We *could* convert it to CoffeeScript manually, but there's a neat utility that we can use to convert JavaScript to CoffeeScript automatically. It's named, appropriately, `js2coffee`, and it's available as an npm module.

 The `js2coffee` utility is also available as a web tool at `http://js2coffee.org/`. You can paste code into a text box and see it immediately converted. This is very helpful if you need to quickly convert a snippet of code!

Let's install the npm module. Use the following command:

```
npm install -g js2coffee
```

 If you see a permissions error, use `sudo` to run this command.

Now we can convert our `.js` files with the following commands:

```
js2coffee app.js > app.coffee
js2coffee routes/index.js > routes/index.coffee
js2coffee routes/user.js > routes/user.coffee
```

Make sure to delete `app.js`, `routes/index.js`, and `routes/user.js` when we're done converting them. We can look over the converted files and tweak them by hand if necessary, but in general, `js2coffee` does a very nice job of generating idiomatic CoffeeScript. For example, `routes/user.coffee` now looks like this:

```
#
# * GET home page.
#
exports.index = (req, res) ->
  res.render "index",
    title: "Ian's Pet Shop"
```

That file is pulled in by `app.coffee`:

```
routes = require("./routes")
```

This is almost identical to the way we would require a file in JavaScript. Even more impressively, this would still work if we were requiring a CoffeeScript file *from* a JavaScript file, or vice versa. As long as we either run our project with the `coffee` command or `require("coffee-script")` early in the file, CoffeeScript will hook into the Node module system so that it will automatically resolve, compile, and use `.coffee` files if no `.js` file exists. This all makes it very easy to use a mixture of JavaScript and CoffeeScript in a Node application. This is good news, because even if your project contains only CoffeeScript, the dependencies are almost certain to contain JavaScript.

Running our application

Starting our server is very easy! Instead of using the `node` command, we'll simply substitute `coffee`:

```
coffee app.coffee
```

Just as before, our application will now be available at `http://localhost:3000/`.

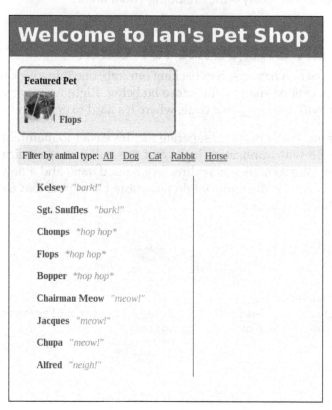

We also used the supervisor tool in *Chapter 10, Using CoffeeScript in More Places* to watch for changes to our files and restart the server to automatically reflect our changes. This too is very easy to accomplish with CoffeeScript source:

```
supervisor app.coffee
```

Supervisor has support for CoffeeScript built-in, so it recognizes the .coffee extension and knows to use the coffee command to run the server. It will now also watch for changes to any files in the source directory with the .coffee extension, in addition to .js files.

Thanks to the require magic we saw earlier, most Node modules will interoperate with a CoffeeScript project without any extra work at all. However, tools that work directly with files (such as supervisor scripts and testing tools) need a little extra code to support CoffeeScript files. Some, like supervisor, automatically support it. Others will need to be passed a special command-line parameter or be otherwise configured to be aware of .coffee files. If you can't figure out how to use your favorite tool with CoffeeScript, contact the author and ask if there is a way to support it. Just remember to ask nicely — they're doing you a favor!

Adding an endpoint for data

Now that we've got a dynamic server backing our app, one thing we can do to improve our application is handle the data a bit better. Right now, we simply throw the list of pets in with the rest of the code, where it's hard to get at and hard to modify.

First, let's move our list of pets to a separate file. It's easier to maintain the data when it isn't mixed with application logic, and this will provide a nice separation of concerns for later. We'll create a new directory named data and a new file named data/pets.coffee. This file will contain our entire list of pets that used to be in assets/js/animal.coffee:

```
module.exports = [
  name: "Kelsey"
  type: "dog"
  age: 2
  breed: "Labrador"
  description: "A sweet and loyal dog. Loves to play fetch.
    Sometimes drinks out of the toilet."
#, ...
```

We're using the Node `module.exports` declaration here and assigning to it the value of the entire array. It declares that requiring this file will expose this array to other files. Let's do that now. We're going to create a simple route for our data. We'll build a single endpoint to provide all the pets as a JSON response. Create a file named `routes/pets.coffee`:

```
petData = require '../data/pets'
# List all pets as JSON
exports.list = (req, res) ->
  res.send petData
```

First we require our data file. Now `petData` holds the array of pet information, since that's what `data/pets.coffee` exposes. Next we define our route. In Express, routes are simple functions that take **request** and **response** objects as arguments. We expose this route as `list` so that it is accessible to our application. The body of our route is extremely simple, thanks to Express. `res.send` instructs the server to send data in the response. As a convenience, Express will helpfully recognize when it is given a data structure (instead of a string) and will automatically send a JSON response. We simply send the whole array we pulled from our data file.

Now we need to add this new route to our application configuration. We'll add a few lines to `app.coffee`. We'll require our route file at the top of `app.coffee`:

```
pets = require("./routes/pets")
```

Then near the bottom, we'll instruct the server that any requests to `/pets` should be sent to that route for handling:

```
app.get "/", routes.index
app.get "/users", user.list
app.get "/pets", pets.list
```

That's all we need on the server side! If we visit `http://localhost:3000/pets` in our browser, we should see the JSON data displayed in raw format on the screen.

Now we'll update our client-side code to use this new server data source. Let's edit our `loadSeedData` function in `assets/js/animal.coffee`.

We'll use Reqwest again to make an AJAX request, this time to our own /pets endpoint. This request won't run into same-origin restrictions, so we can use a regular JSON data type instead of JSONP.

```
reqwest
  url: "/pets"
  type: "json"
  success: (response) =>
    animals = for animal in response
      @fromHash animal
```

Upon receiving a response, we can build Animal objects out of it just as before, using our fromHash constructor. To make sure we have access to this context, we declare the success callback using a fat arrow.

When we try to place this code in the loadSeedData function, we can see a problem. The function expects to return an array of data, but our web request is asynchronous. We need to return from the function, but we don't yet have the data to give to the caller! It's time to turn loadSeedData into an asynchronous function itself. We'll modify it to take one argument, a callback:

```
@loadSeedData: (callback) ->
  reqwest
    url: "/pets"
    type: "json"
    success: (response) =>
      animals = for animal in response
        @fromHash animal
      callback animals
```

When we receive a response, we invoke the callback function, passing it the processed list of pets. Our caller will have to wait until then to work with the data.

Since we've changed how that function behaves, we'll also need to change the place it is called, setup.coffee. We'll remove the animals property from the configuration hash:

```
shop = {
  owner: new Person "Ian"
  featured: [ "Chupa", "Kelsey", "Flops" ]
}
```

Now, instead of constructing the views right away, we'll fire off our asynchronous `loadSeedData` call, and we'll wait until our callback is invoked before we render the page.

```
Animal.loadSeedData (animals) ->
  petViews = (new PetView pet for pet in animals)
  petListView = new PetListView petViews, shop.featured
  mainView = new ShopView shop.owner, petListView
  mainView.render()
```

The loop to construct `PetView` objects is now using the `animals` variable passed into the callback from our asynchronous web request.

Everything is ready! Let's reload the primary application page at `http://localhost:3000/`. Everything should look much the same as before. If you watch carefully, you might catch a brief moment where the page isn't populated as it waits for the data it needs.

Using a database

We've successfully moved our application's data to an encapsulated endpoint, which is great. Now that we've done that, we can start thinking about making that data dynamic. Right now it's stored in a static code file. This is fine when none of the data needs to change, but if we want our application to be interactive, we'll need a way to work with the data. It's time to use a database.

There are many powerful database solutions available, from SQL options such as MySQL and Postgres, to a newer breed of NoSQL engines such as MongoDB and CouchDB, plus simple key-value stores such as Redis and Riak. Almost all popular database engines have drivers available for Node. However, we're going to use a simpler option. We'll be using a database named **nStore**, which is written entirely in JavaScript and uses a simple file store. This means we won't need to fuss with installing extra software, running services, and compiling drivers. Instead, we can install a simple Node module and focus on building our application.

 The nStore documentation is available on the project page at `https://github.com/creationix/nstore`.

We'll add the `nstore` module to our `package.json` to mark it as a dependency of our application:

```
"dependencies": {
  "express": "3.2.4",
  "connect-assets": "2.4.x",
  "coffee-script": "1.x",
  "nstore":
    "https://github.com/iangreenleaf/nstore/archive/
      coffeescript_book.tar.gz",
  "ejs": "*"
}
```

 We're using a special feature of npm here. Given a URL to a package tarball, npm will install it directly. This allows us to use a patched version of this library without publishing it to the central npm package repository.

Then install the package as specified:

npm install

Now in `routes/pets.coffee`, instead of reading the pet data from a file we'll request it from the database. First we'll require the `nstore` package:

```
nStore = require 'nstore'
nStore = nStore.extend require('nstore/query')()
```

That second line is specified by the nStore documentation. It adds some simple query language to the nStore client that will allow us to select more than one record at a time.

nStore was designed with JavaScript in mind, but as we've seen before, integrating with CoffeeScript should prove no trouble at all. Let's update the list action to read records from the database. First we need to initialize the database from a file.

```
exports.list = (req, res) ->
  nStore.new 'data/pets.db', (err, petsDB) ->
```

This creates a new database client reading from `data/pets.db`. This function follows the Node convention for asynchronous behavior: the last argument passed to the function is a callback that will be invoked when the database is ready. This callback takes two arguments, an error (which is empty as long as everything went well) and a database client.

Now that we have a client to the database, we can request all the pet records and send them as a response:

```
exports.list = (req, res) ->
  nStore.new 'data/pets.db', (err, petsDB) ->
    petsDB.all (err, result) ->
      res.send (pet for key, pet of result)
```

The `petsDB.all` method once again takes a callback as the last (and only) argument. This callback will be invoked when the query finishes, with either an error or (hopefully) a result from the database.

The `result` object is keyed by id, like this:

```
{
  19av4ojo: { name: "Kelsey", … }
  1nv59mto: { name: "Flops", … }
}
```

We'll massage this data slightly to get it into the format that our client-side code already expects. We simply convert the keyed object into an ordinary array of pets. With this done, we can once again make use of the `res.send` shortcut to easily send a JSON response.

With this route logic written, it's easy to see how CoffeeScript will improve our Node experience. Node code tends to involve many, many callbacks, and nobody does anonymous functions better than CoffeeScript. The clean, simple function syntax makes it much easier to read through asynchronous code and focus on the important parts without sorting through parentheses and braces. Compare our code to the JavaScript examples in the nStore documentation, and I think you'll agree with me that there's a clear winner!

Handling errors

Before continuing, we should put some error handling in place. By Node convention, many asynchronous callbacks take an error as a first argument. If everything went well, this argument will be null. If something bad happened during the asynchronous operation, this argument will contain an error object with an error message and information about the failure. It's a good idea to check these error arguments and abort sensibly if they are present.

We have a couple of places where the database calls may fail. For right now, any of these would be an *unexpected* failure, so we can define generic behavior that applies to all of them. Let's add a new private function to `routes/pets.coffee`.

```
_fail = (err, res) ->
  console.log err
  res.send 500
```

This is the simplest error handling that's still useful. It logs the error to the console for debugging purposes, and returns a 500 response code to the browser. We'll use this in our route in the places an error might crop up.

```
exports.list = (req, res) ->
  nStore.new 'data/pets.db', (err, petsDB) ->
    return _fail err, res if err?
    petsDB.all (err, result) ->
      return _fail err, res if err?
      res.send (pet for key, pet of result)
```

This ensures that our application will behave in a reasonable manner if something goes wrong, and that we'll have the records to help us track it down. We can update the body of `_fail` later if we wish to add more complex logging or any other generic failure actions.

Using a Cakefile

We've gotten a little ahead of ourselves. We upgraded our application to use data from a database, but right now our database doesn't exist! While we might build some sort of import system or data entry interface to add records to our application in production, during development it's nice to be able to easily add a set of **seed** data. We already have this seed data, we just need a way to put it into our database.

CoffeeScript provides a simple but effective solution to these sorts of problems: **Cakefiles**. Cakefiles are inspired by the venerable Makefiles, the build system for C and friends. The premise of a Makefile and its variants (Ruby users will also be familiar with Rakefiles) is simple: it consists of various tasks which can be invoked individually from the command line. Each task definition contains instructions that will be run when the task is run. In a Cakefile, the task definitions and bodies are all written in CoffeeScript.

Think of a Cakefile as a very simple command-line interface to various tasks for our application. It's a great place to store helpful snippets of code that don't belong in the application itself, but still come in handy on a regular basis.

Writing a Cake task

We'll create a new file named simply `Cakefile`, at the root of our application. Once again, we'll require the `nstore` package at the top of the file. We'll also require our seed data from its file in the `data` directory.

```
nStore = require 'nstore'
petSeedData = require './data/pets'
```

Now we'll define our Cake task, giving an invocation and a short description:

```
task "db:seed", "Seed the database", ->
```

The body of the task will look much like the other work we've done with our database:

```
task "db:seed", "Seed the database", ->
  nStore.new 'data/pets.db', (err, petsDB) ->
    return console.log err if err?
    for pet in petSeedData
      petsDB.save null, pet, (err) ->
        console.log err if err?
```

We create the database client, just as before. This time, we loop through each entry in our seed data and use `save` to persist the record to the database. The first argument to `save` is an optional key. If we had an existing key that uniquely identified the records, we could use that, but since we don't, we'll leave it as `null` and let nStore automatically generate a key.

Now that we've defined our cake task, we can run it from the command line:

cake db:seed

If we load our application in a browser, we should see the pet list, much the same as always.

More Cake tasks

To help our development work further, let's add one more Cake task that clears out the database and re-seeds it. This is useful if we make changes to the structure of the data, or screw up the existing data and wish to simply load a fresh copy of our seeds. We'll define this task after the first one in our `Cakefile`:

```
task "db:reset", "Reset the database to a clean development
  state", ->
  nStore.new 'data/pets.db', (err, petsDB) ->
    return console.log err if err?
```

```
petsDB.clear (err) ->
  return console.log err if err?
  invoke "db:seed"
```

We use nStore's `clear` method to empty the database. When that is finished (and calls the asynchronous callback), we are ready to re-seed the database. We make use of Cake's `invoke` function, which runs our previously defined Cake task.

Now we can reset the database with just a single command!

cake db:reset

Making our application interactive

We've improved our application to be fed data from a database. Now it's time for the payoff—we can let users interact with our application, and their actions can be reflected in our data. We're going to add a feature where customers may buy a pet they like, directly through the website! We've got some implementation work to do.

To send a request to buy a pet, we'll need the pet ID that's used as the database key. This is returned when we query all the records, but so far we've been dropping it from the results we send to the browser. We'll update the data in `routes/pets.coffee`:

```
exports.list = (req, res) ->
  nStore.new 'data/pets.db', (err, petsDB) ->
    return _fail err, res if err?
    petsDB.all (err, result) ->
      return _fail err, res if err?
      response = for key, pet of result
        pet.id = key
        pet
      res.send response
```

We've added `id` as a property to each of the JSON objects we send out. Now our client-side code can use this ID to identify which pet is being purchased.

We'll add a small button at the bottom of the pet view.

```
formattedDescription: ->
  #... +
    "<div id='extra_links' class='more'></div>" +
    @purchaseForm()
```

```
purchaseForm: ->
  "<div id='purchase'>" +
    "<form method='POST' action='/pets/#{@pet.id}/buy'>" +
      "<input type='submit' value='Buy' />" +
    "</form>" +
  "</div>"
```

After reloading our application, we can see this button when we choose a pet from the list.

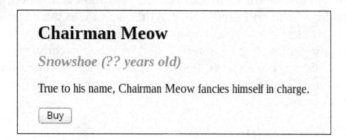

In production we might collect payment information here or have the customer fill out a reservation form, but for now we'll take their word for it and mark the pet as sold right away. We're submitting the form to /pets/:id/buy, a URL that we haven't built a route for yet. Let's add a matcher for that URL in app.coffee:

```
app.post "/pets/:id/buy", pets.buy
```

Notice that we've used app.post to instruct Express to expect a POST request here, rather than the usual GET request. The :id part of the URL is a special syntax that tells Express to expect a value there that will be made available to our handler later. We're handling requests to this endpoint with pets.buy, so let's add that route to routes/pets.coffee.

```
exports.buy = (req, res) ->
  nStore.new 'data/pets.db', (err, petsDB) ->
    return _fail err, res if err?
```

So far, so good. We've initialized our database client, and reused our _fail function from the previous section to abort gracefully if anything goes wrong. Now we need to find the record for the ID sent in the request.

```
petsDB.get req.params.id, (err, pet) ->
  return _fail err, res if err?
```

We use petsDB.get to request a single record. The ID that we need was in the URL of this request. Thanks to the URL matcher we gave to Express, the value is now available in the req.params object.

Now it's just a matter of marking this pet as sold and persisting that to the database.

```
pet.sold = true
petsDB.save pet.id, pet, (err, result) ->
  return _fail err, res if err?
  res.render "purchase_confirmation", pet
```

This time, we *do* pass a key as the first argument to save. We want to make sure this updates the old record instead of creating a new record. The save function, as per convention, will invoke the callback once the operation is finished, so we wait until then to render a page and send a successful response to the browser. This is a glimpse of what makes the fully-asynchronous nature of Node applications so useful—we've waited for several different I/O operations to complete, but the event loop has never needed to burn cycles. Instead, it simply invokes a callback at the appropriate time, and we send a response from *within* the final callback to let the browser know we're finished.

Here's the whole route handler function all at once:

```
exports.buy = (req, res) ->
  nStore.new 'data/pets.db', (err, petsDB) ->
    return _fail err, res if err?
    petsDB.get req.params.id, (err, pet) ->
      return _fail err, res if err?
      pet.sold = true
      petsDB.save pet.id, pet, (err, result) ->
        return _fail err, res if err?
        res.render "purchase_confirmation", pet
```

Once again, we can see how much CoffeeScript's readable syntax improves this code. Even though there are multiple levels of nested asynchronous callbacks, it remains easy to follow, and easy to tell which lines are at which level of nesting, thanks to the clean function syntax and whitespace-based function grouping.

We have one last thing to do: build a confirmation screen to render once the purchase has gone through. We'll create a new file at `views/purchase_confirmation.ejs`. This will show a very simple confirmation screen with instructions on claiming the newly-purchased pet.

```
<!DOCTYPE html>
<html>
  <head>
    <meta charset="UTF-8">
```

```
        <title>Purchase confirmation - The Pet Shop</title>
        <%- css("style") %>
      </head>
      <body>
        <h1>Purchase confirmed</h1>
        <p>Thanks for adopting <%= name %>!</p>
        <p>Please visit our shop soon to pick up your new
        <%= type %>.</p>
      </body>
    </html>
```

We passed the `pet` object to `res.render` when we called it from our route handler. This set the properties of that object as local variables that are now available to our template. This allows us to personalize the confirmation with the pet name and type by using the EJS `<%= ... %>` syntax to insert a value.

Let's choose a pet from the list and click on **Buy**. We should be taken to a confirmation screen, and the pet will be marked as sold in our database.

Seeing the results

We've set our app up to dynamically update the database, but right now it's hard to see it working. Let's make it a little more apparent. Once someone has bought a pet, we should no longer show that pet in the list. Let's update the data returned by our `pets.list` route so that it only shows unsold pets.

Luckily, nStore provides some query options that will work great for this type of filtering. Rather than using `petsDB.all` to retrieve all records from the database, we'll use `find` to be more selective.

```
exports.list = (req, res) ->
  nStore.new 'data/pets.db', (err, petsDB) ->
    return _fail err, res if err?
    petsDB.find "sold !=": true, (err, result) ->
      return _fail err, res if err?
      response = for key, pet of result
        pet.id = key
        pet
      res.send response
```

The key and value that we pass to that function indicates that we want all records for which `sold` is not `true`. Everything else in this route can stay the same, and now that we've adjusted the data we're serving up, our client-side code should adjust automatically.

If we reload the main application page, any pets that we have marked as sold will no longer show up in the pet list.

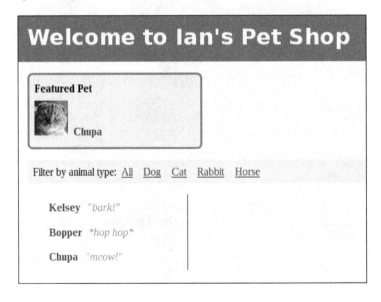

That's it! We're all done! Our application is now capable of serving and updating data dynamically, thanks to a database and the Express framework. And best of all, we're using CoffeeScript on both ends!

Summary

Amazingly, that's all you need to know about CoffeeScript and Node. There's plenty more to learn about the Node ecosystem, but with your expert knowledge of the CoffeeScript language, you'll find it quite easy to interact with new server-side modules using our favorite language. We've seen just how easy it is to use CoffeeScript and JavaScript side by side in both client and server environments, so you're ready for anything the future holds.

In this chapter, we learned how to:

- Write our server-side Node project in CoffeeScript
- Integrate our CoffeeScript code in a Node framework like Express
- Call out seamlessly to JavaScript modules such as `nstore`
- Use Cakefiles to modularize common development tasks

You've done it! You've reached the end of the line! We started with the very basics of CoffeeScript, and now we're writing idiomatic, beautiful code. Not only have we learned the language, we've learned how to refactor and use classes and inheritance. We've learned how to tame asynchronous operations, compile CoffeeScript from our favorite web application frameworks, debug natively, and now how to write our server code in CoffeeScript as well! And we've put it all to use building a functional web application that just happens to serve up cat pictures.

Our work here is done, but your adventures in CoffeeScript may be only beginning.

Index

source maps, Firefox developer tools
  about 171
  application state, inspecting 172-174
  debugger, using 174-178
splats
  about 87
  arguments, accepting with 87
  functions, invoking with 88
  using, in application 89-92
standalone executable
  used, for installing Node.js on Windows 12
state
  maintaining, with object properties 98
statements 27
static methods 103
string interpolation
  about 52
  using, in application 53
Sublime Text 2 21
switch statements
  about 63, 65
  using, in application 65

T

TextMate 20
then method 159
third-party library
  refactoring 152, 153
  using 151

top-level display logic 124, 125
Try CoffeeScript tool
  URL 26

U

Underscore.js 39
unless statement 33, 34

V

values
  assigning, conditionally 72, 73
  existence, verifying 69, 70
variables
  about 27, 28
  functions, assigning to 55
Vim 21

W

watch expression 176
web application
  starting 22, 23
when keyword 41
work
  saving, with memoization 135

Thank you for buying
CoffeeScript Application Development

About Packt Publishing

Packt, pronounced 'packed', published its first book "*Mastering phpMyAdmin for Effective MySQL Management*" in April 2004 and subsequently continued to specialize in publishing highly focused books on specific technologies and solutions.

Our books and publications share the experiences of your fellow IT professionals in adapting and customizing today's systems, applications, and frameworks. Our solution based books give you the knowledge and power to customize the software and technologies you're using to get the job done. Packt books are more specific and less general than the IT books you have seen in the past. Our unique business model allows us to bring you more focused information, giving you more of what you need to know, and less of what you don't.

Packt is a modern, yet unique publishing company, which focuses on producing quality, cutting-edge books for communities of developers, administrators, and newbies alike. For more information, please visit our website: www.packtpub.com.

About Packt Open Source

In 2010, Packt launched two new brands, Packt Open Source and Packt Enterprise, in order to continue its focus on specialization. This book is part of the Packt Open Source brand, home to books published on software built around Open Source licences, and offering information to anybody from advanced developers to budding web designers. The Open Source brand also runs Packt's Open Source Royalty Scheme, by which Packt gives a royalty to each Open Source project about whose software a book is sold.

Writing for Packt

We welcome all inquiries from people who are interested in authoring. Book proposals should be sent to author@packtpub.com. If your book idea is still at an early stage and you would like to discuss it first before writing a formal book proposal, contact us; one of our commissioning editors will get in touch with you.

We're not just looking for published authors; if you have strong technical skills but no writing experience, our experienced editors can help you develop a writing career, or simply get some additional reward for your expertise.

CoffeeScript Programming with jQuery, Rails, and Node.js

ISBN: 978-1-84951-958-8   Paperback: 140 pages

Learn CoffeeScript programming with the three most popular web technologies around

1. Learn CoffeeScript, a small and elegant language that compiles to JavaScript and will make your life as a web developer better

2. Explore the syntax of the language and see how it improves and enhances JavaScript

3. Build three example applications in CoffeeScript step by step

JavaScript Unit Testing

ISBN: 978-1-78216-062-5   Paperback: 190 pages

Your comprehensive and pratical guide to efficiently performing and automating JavaScript unit testing

1. Learn and understand, using practical examples, synchronous and asynchronous JavaScript unit testing

2. Cover the most popular JavaScript Unit Testing Frameworks including Jasmine, YUITest, QUnit, and JsTestDriver

3. Automate and integrate your JavaScript Unit Testing for ease and efficiency

Please check **www.PacktPub.com** for information on our titles

iPhone JavaScript Cookbook

ISBN: 978-1-84969-108-6   Paperback: 328 pages

Clear and practical recipes for building web applicationa using JavaScript and AJAX without having to learn Objective-C or Cocoa

1. Build web applications for iPhone with a native look feel using only JavaScript, CSS, and XHTML

2. Develop applications faster using frameworks

3. Integrate videos, sound, and images into your iPhone applications

4. Work with data using SQL and AJAX

Learning JavaScriptMVC

ISBN: 978-1-78216-020-5   Paperback: 124 pages

Learn to build well-structured JavaScript web applications using JavaScriptMVC

1. Install JavaScriptMVC in three different ways, including installing using Vagrant and Chef

2. Document your JavaScript codebase and generate searchable API documentation

3. Test your codebase and application as well as learning how to integrate tests with the continuous integration tool, Jenkins

Please check **www.PacktPub.com** for information on our titles